WILD BIRD GUIDES

Northern Cardinal

Gary Ritchison

STACKPOLE
BOOKS

For Tammy and Brandon

Published by
STACKPOLE BOOKS
5067 Ritter Road
Mechanicsburg, PA 17055

Printed in Hong Kong

10   9   8   7   6   5   4   3   2   1

First edition

Cover design by Tracy Patterson

Cover photo by Richard Day/Daybreak Imagery

Library of Congress Cataloging-in-Publication Data

Ritchison, Gary.
      Northern cardinal / Gary Ritchison. — 1st ed.
          p.   cm. — (Wild bird guides)
      Includes bibliographical references (p.   ).
      ISBN 0-8117-3100-6 (pbk.)
      1. Northern cardinal.   I. Title. II. Series
   QL696.P2438R57   1997
   598.8'83—dc20

                                      96-44268
                                        CIP

Contents

Acknowledgments

The efforts of many ornithologists and ethologists are summarized in the text of this book. Although the names of these individuals are listed in the References, I'd like to especially thank several whose publications, dissertations, or theses were particularly useful: Glenn W. Kinser, Robert E. Lemon, Douglas D. Dow, Tamatha S. Filliater, Randall Breitwisch, Paul M. Nealen, Ann Richmond, Mary E. Andersen, Richard N. Conner, Mary F. Willson, and Geoffrey E. Hill. Many thanks also to those who have worked with me to learn more about the behavior and ecology of Northern Cardinals: M. Katherine Omer, Paul H. Klatt, David B. McElroy, Debra S. Pressman, and Sunni Lawless. Our work with cardinals was supported by the Eastern Kentucky University Research Committee, Kentucky NSF EPSCoR, and the Frank M. Chapman Fund of the American Museum of Natural History. For providing the many excellent photographs that accompany the text, I thank Maslowski Photo, Bill Dyuck, Leonard Lee Rue III, Jim Roetzel, Richard Day, Ron Morreim, Deborah Allen, Steve Bentsen, Robert Campbell, Gary W. Carter, D. Dvorak, Jr., Grady H. Harrison, Jr., G. C. Kelley, Rich Kirchner, Stephen Kirkpatrick, Gerard Lemmo, Ron Levy, Doug Locke, Charles W. Melton, C. Allan Morgan, James H. Robinson, Gregory K. Scott, John Serrao, Tom J. Ulrich, Tom Vezo, William K. Vinje, and J. R. Woodward. Finally, special thanks to Merrill J. Frydendall for stimulating and encouraging my interest in bird behavior, to my parents, Kenneth and Leona, for always being there, and to my wife and son, Tammy and Brandon, for their love and support.

An Introduction

"In richness of plumage, elegance of motion, and strength of song, this species surpasses all its kindred." These are the words used by John James Audubon to describe the Northern Cardinal. Other, more recent, writers have expressed similar feelings. Arthur Cleveland Bent, a well-known bird biographer of this century, wrote: "In the Cardinal we have a rare combination of good qualities, brilliant plumage, a rich and pleasing voice, beneficial food habits, and devotion to its mate and family. Many of our best singers are not clothed in brilliant plumage, and many of our handsomest birds are not gifted musicians." It is obvious that the sentiments expressed by Audubon and Bent are still shared by many people because Northern Cardinals are certainly among the most popular of all birds.

Northern Cardinals were formally described by Swedish biologist Carolus Linnaeus in 1758 and given the scientific name *Loxia cardinalis.* The cardinal was so named for the cardinals in the Roman Catholic Church, who wore red robes and hats. *Loxia* is derived from the Greek *loxos* and means "crosswise." There is nothing crosswise about cardinals, but apparently Linnaeus felt that cardinals were closely related to another red bird, the Red Crossbill. Subsequently, taxonomists realized that these two species were not that closely related, and in 1838, the scientific name of the cardinal was changed to *Cardinalis virginianus.* The specific name *virginianus* refers to the state of Virginia, where cardinals are a common species. In 1918, the scientific name was changed again—this time to *Richmondena cardinalis,* in honor of U.S. ornithologist Charles Wallace Richmond. The last name change occurred in 1983, when cardinals were assigned their current scientific name of *Cardinalis cardinalis* and the common name was changed from cardinal to Northern Cardinal. There are seven other species called cardinals, only one of which, the Vermilion Cardinal, is in the same genus as the Northern Cardinal, and referring to *Cardinalis cardinalis* as simply the cardinal could create uncertainty about which species is being discussed. Because all the other species of cardinals are found in South America, the modifier Northern is appropriate.

Adult cardinals are 7.5 to 8.5 inches (19 to 21.5 centimeters) long and weigh about 1.4 to 1.8 ounces (40 to 50 grams), with no significant differences in the size of males and females. Males and females do, however, differ in appearance. Both have a crest and a stout orange-red bill, but males are bright red with a black face, and females are buff-brown with dark red in the wings, tail, and crest. The back, rump, upper tail coverts, and wing coverts of males are somewhat duller because the feathers have grayish edges. Females have a face mask, but it is sooty or grayish black rather than black. The legs and feet of males and females are dark flesh colored, and the iris is deep brown. Cardinals are the same size and have the same appearance throughout their range, with little or no geographic variation.

Young male and female cardinals do not attain adult plumage until their first fall and winter. Before that time, their plumage is decidedly female-like. Cardinals with this juvenal plumage are dark brown above and brown or reddish brown below. The crest, forehead, wings, and tail are dark brown mixed with brick red, and there is a trace of a dark mask on the chin or lores (the area between the bill and the eyes).

Young cardinals also have black bills rather than the orange-red of adults. The black bill gradually becomes orange-red over several months. Young cardinals usually develop adultlike plumage and bills by three or four months after hatching, or by December at the latest).

Among many well-known species of birds, such as the American Robin, House Wren, and Northern Mockingbird, males and females are similar in appearance. But this is not the case with the cardinal. Species in which males and females differ in size or appearance are said to be sexually dimorphic, and species like the cardinal, in which males and females differ in coloration, are called dichromatic. Female cardinals, like the females of many other species, have relatively dull plumage, and it is generally assumed that such plumage reduces visibility and, therefore, reduces the chance of being spotted by a predator. Such camouflage may be particularly important for females, which spend long hours on their nests incubating eggs and brooding young. In contrast, male cardinals are bright red and, presumably, more easily spotted by predators. Despite this major disadvantage, the maintenance of such bright plumage suggests that it also provides important advantages.

Bright red plumage may aid male cardinals in interactions with other males (intrasexual advantages), with females (intersexual advantages), or with both. Plumage variation has been found to offer such advantages in other species of birds. For example, male House Sparrows have black patches, or badges, on the throat and breast, and several studies have revealed that males with larger badges tend to be dominant over males with smaller badges and are also preferred as mates by females. Thus, among House Sparrows, male quality appears to be correlated with badge size, and males with larger badges obtain both intra- and intersexual advantages.

Male cardinals also exhibit variation in plumage—specifically, in the quality and quantity of bright red breast plumage. Although not yet convincingly demonstrated, it is possible that those males with brighter, redder breast plumage do better in interactions with other males and are also more attractive to females. Thus, other male and female cardinals may be able to judge a male's status or quality by examining his breast plumage. For such a status signaling system to work, however, plumage quality must be a true indicator of male quality. In other words, lower-ranking or lower-quality males must not be able to "cheat" by developing brighter plumage than higher-ranking or higher-quality males.

Male and female cardinals, and other species of birds with red plumage, get their red coloration from pigments called carotenoids. Birds cannot synthesize carotenoid pigments but must obtain them from their food. Carotenoids are present in a variety of foods, particularly those that exhibit orange or red coloration. Ingested carotenoids are deposited in feathers during new feather development (during molt), and the amount of carotenoids ingested influences plumage coloration.

Male House Finches exhibit individual variation in coloration, with their plumage ranging from pale yellow to bright red. Experiments have revealed that this variation results from differences in carotenoid intake. Male House Finches that eat more foods containing carotenoids at the time of molt have brighter, redder plumage. Although similar experiments have not yet been conducted with cardinals, it is likely that individual variation among males (and, to a lesser degree, females) in the redness of their plumage is also the result of differences in diet.

It is possible that the quality of a male cardinal's red plumage is linked to the quality of his diet. This is potentially significant, because the quality of a bird's diet is a reflection of several important characteristics, including competitive ability, foraging skills, coordination, vision, and disease resistance. In other words, a better-quality individual may have a better-quality diet and, as a result, better-quality plumage. Among male cardinals, therefore, bright red plumage— particularly bright red breast plumage—may be a signal of quality. If, in the distant past, some female cardinals displayed a preference for slightly more colorful, redder males, then, assuming a correlation between plumage and male quality, these females would have benefited because they were pairing with higher-quality males. Pairing with higher-quality males would likely have resulted in increased reproductive success for females, because such males would probably have had better territories with more necessary resources, such as food and nest sites, and might have been better parents. Improved reproductive success, in turn, would have reinforced female preferences for brighter, redder plumage. Over many generations, as females tended to select such mates, male cardinals would have become progressively redder. And brighter, redder males would have benefited, despite possible increases in predation rates, because they were more likely to be chosen as mates by females. It is equally possible that males became progressively brighter and redder over time because brighter, redder males were more successful in interactions with duller males and were able to obtain better-quality territories or greater access to food during the winter. Improved access to food or better territories would have translated into better physical condition and greater reproductive success, spreading genetic tendencies for brighter, redder plumage through the population.

Female cardinals also exhibit plumage variation, with individuals differing in the quantity and quality of red feathers on the upper breast, crest, eyebrow, face, and sides. Females also vary in bill color. This variation in female ornamentation does not appear to be correlated with age. It is possible, although not yet demonstrated, that this variation in female appearance is correlated with some other quality, such as fertility. That is, females with brighter ornamentation may be in better condition, because the brighter appearance may indicate a better diet, and they may, on average, produce larger clutches. This is yet to be determined, and it is possible that there are other explanations for the observed variation in female ornamentation.

There is much more to male and female Northern Cardinals than their attractive plumage. Like other living organisms, individual Northern Cardinals are products of the evolutionary process and constantly do their best to survive and reproduce. The efforts of amateur and professional ornithologists and wildlife photographers have revealed many interesting details about the lives of Northern Cardinals. In the following chapters, various aspects of cardinal morphology, physiology, ecology, and behavior are explored.

2

Taxonomy and Distribution

The Northern Cardinal is one of approximately 9,600 known species of birds. Each species has a characteristic appearance and geographic range and, most importantly, is reproductively isolated from other species. Species that have broad geographic distributions are commonly divided into subspecies, because groups of individuals separated for some time from other such groups often develop slightly different characteristics. Northern Cardinals have been divided into seven subspecies. Although subspecies may exhibit minor variation in size and appearance, most other aspects of their behavior and ecology are similar.

11

The genus *Cardinalis* includes Northern Cardinals; Pyrrhuloxias (*Cardinalis sinatus*), at right, a species found throughout Mexico and the southwestern United States; and Vermilion Cardinals (*Cardinalis phoeniceus*), a species found in Colombia and Venezuela. Pyrrhuloxias are similar to Northern cardinals in size and have red crests, but they are grayer and have an abruptly curved upper mandible. The songs of these two species are also similar. For example, their songs consist of repetitions of sounds or syllables, and in some areas, the syllables used by the two species are similar. However, experiments revealed that individuals exposed to the songs of both species had a greater response to the songs of their own species. Observations also indicate that the territories of cardinals and Pyrrhuloxias overlap. Cardinals defend territories only against other cardinals, and Pyrrhuloxias defend only against other Pyrrhuloxias. Thus, despite the similarities in appearance and singing behavior, there appears to be little interaction between these species during the breeding season. During the nonbreeding season, cardinals and Pyrrhuloxias can sometimes be found in the same flocks, often with other species as well.

The Vermilion Cardinal of South America is limited in distribution to the Caribbean coasts of northeastern Colombia and northern Venezuela, where it occupies dense thorny thickets and desert scrub. Vermilion Cardinals are similar in appearance to Northern Cardinals. Both males and females have stout bills and long, pointed crests. Males are mostly bright rosy red, with dusky gray edges on their wing and tail feathers. Females are sandy gray above but have a rosy red crest. The underparts are sandy brown, and the tail feathers are tinged with dark red. Although it is not a well-studied species, the behavior of the Vermilion Cardinal is thought to be similar to that of the Northern Cardinal.

Northern Cardinals also bear some resemblance to other, less closely related, species. Male Scarlet (shown here) and Summer Tanagers have red plumage, but unlike cardinals, male Scarlet Tanagers have black wings. In addition, neither tanager species has a crest, black plumage on the chin and lores, or a conical beak. Male Red and White-winged Crossbills are also largely red, but both have black wings (with white wing bars in the case of male White-winged Crossbills) and tails, and their bills cross at the tip.

Groups of related genera are placed in common subfamilies and families. Northern Cardinals belong to the subfamily Cardinalinae, along with a number of related species, including the grosbeaks and buntings. Families consist of a number of related subfamilies, and the cardinal family, Emberizidae, includes the warblers, blackbirds, orioles, tanagers, and sparrows. Emberizids, along with many other families, are members of the order Passeriformes, the perching birds.

Northern Cardinals can be found throughout the eastern United States, bounded on the east by the Atlantic Ocean and on the south by the Gulf of Mexico. The northern limit of their range extends west from Maine through southern Ontario to North Dakota. This northern limit may be determined by temperature, with cardinals found only where the average minimum January temperature is 5 degrees Fahrenheit (–15 degrees Celsius). Snow cover may also be a factor. The northern edge of the cardinal's range in Ontario appears to correspond to an area east of the Great Lakes that typically receives abundant snowfall (64 to 80 inches [1.6 to 2 meters] per year).

Because cardinals are largely ground feeders, deep snow probably hinders their ability to obtain food. As a result, in the northern parts of their range, heavy snowfall may induce cardinals to move into towns, where more food might be available. Winter feeding by humans at bird feeders probably helps maintain cardinal populations in their northern range.

The western edge of their range extends south from the Dakotas to western Texas, with populations also found in the southern parts of Arizona, New Mexico, and California. Cardinal distribution in the western and south-western United States appears to be limited by moisture, with cardinals typically found only in regions that receive more than sixteen inches (forty-one centimeters) of annual precipitation. Cardinals can also be found throughout much of Mexico (including Baja California) and as far south as Guatemala in Central America. In three other areas—southern California, Bermuda, and Hawaii—Cardinals were introduced by humans. The population in southern California was introduced in Pasadena in 1923 and has not exhibited much expansion. Cardinals were probably introduced to Bermuda by early settlers in about 1700 and became rather common. However, habitat loss and competition with introduced House Sparrows, Starlings, and Kiskadees have substantially reduced the population. Cardinals were released on the islands of Oahu, Kauai, and Hawaii in about 1929 and have since spread to other islands. Cardinals are now common in many lowland areas and residential areas in the Hawaiian Islands.

Over the past hundred years, cardinals have greatly expanded their range. In 1886, cardinals were found only infrequently north of the Ohio River. By 1895, their range extended to the Great Lakes and, by 1910, extended into southern Ontario and the southern Hudson River valley. The first report of cardinals in southern Ontario was in 1896, and they remained rare until about 1910. Cardinal populations in the northeastern United States began increasing dramatically in the 1940s and 1950s. Cardinals first nested in Connecticut around 1943 and in eastern Massachusetts in 1958. In New York, cardinals were breeding in only two of sixty-two counties in 1914, but they were breeding in fifty-nine counties by the early 1970s. Cardinals' expansion west and northwest has generally followed the Mississippi and Missouri Rivers and their tributaries. For example, as of 1934, cardinals were common only in the southern half of Iowa and along the Mississippi and Missouri River valleys. Similarly, cardinals were largely confined to the southeastern portion of Minnesota in 1936. Since the 1930s, cardinals have extended their range across most of Iowa and Minnesota. Trees and other vegetation along rivers probably provided food and cover for dispersing cardinals.

Much of the expansion to the northeast and northwest appears to be the result of dispersal by young cardinals. Such movement by young birds from their birth sites to breeding locations is common and is referred to as natal dispersal. Dispersal does not, however, always result in range expansion. Several factors may have contributed to the successful range expansion of cardinals, including increases in mean annual temperature in the northern portions of their range. Also contributing may have been changes in habitat. Cardinals typically prefer small trees and shrubs (edge habitat), and land-use practices in the Northeast over the last several decades have provided more of this habitat. For example, abandoned agricultural land becomes overgrown with small trees and shrubs, at least for several years, and provides good habitat for cardinals. Also, urban and especially suburban areas often develop better vegetative cover over time, providing suitable habitat for cardinals. Increased food availability could also be a factor. Millions of people are now feeding birds in North America, and it is likely that this supply of food, especially in northern areas, has contributed to the range expansion of cardinals.

A bird's habitat consists of a complex array of living (biotic) and nonliving (abiotic) factors. Among the nonliving factors are such things as temperature and precipitation; living factors include such things as the quantity and quality of various types of food and the type and number of predators. Some authors view habitat selection by birds as an interaction between proximate and ultimate factors. Ultimate factors, such as food and shelter, are essential for survival. Proximate factors, such as terrain, substrate, and the arrangement of the vegetation, attract birds but need not have immediate biological significance.

Some species of birds have very specific habitat requirements. For example, breeding Kirtland's Warblers apparently require large tracts of jack pines about six to eighteen feet tall. Northern Cardinals have much broader habitat requirements. Cardinals can be found in a wide range of habitats, from cities to deciduous forests to cypress swamps to pine plantations. Some investigators have suggested that cardinals require some open fields in their territories for feeding purposes, but others believe that cardinals have little trouble obtaining food in forested areas, from either the forest floor or the canopy. Studies in Michigan revealed that cardinals occupy a diversity of habitats and can be found along marsh edges, in dry upland areas with shrubs and small trees, and in association with humans. Despite this tolerance for a variety of habitats, studies of habitat use have revealed that cardinals do exhibit some preferences. In Tennessee, cardinals selected wooded areas with dense understories and relatively open canopies. Investigators in east Texas found that, although widely distributed, cardinals were more likely to occur in areas with more shrubs and less likely to occur in areas with taller trees and a dense crown.

It appears that cardinals require some shrubs or other dense foliage no more than about ten feet high for both nest sites and, to a lesser degree, foraging. Research has revealed that the size of cardinal territories is negatively correlated with foliage density. In other words, territories are smaller in areas with more shrubs. If shrub foliage is sparse, cardinals increase their territory size to compensate. Males, and perhaps females, probably prefer to have some taller trees as well, to use as singing perches. In general, it appears that, although cardinals require a certain amount of understory foliage (shrubs) for nesting and feeding, the type of vegetation in the rest of their territories can vary greatly. Such flexibility explains why cardinals are found in such a wide variety of habitats.

Cardinals are among the few species of birds that may be as abundant in urban areas as in more natural habitats. A study conducted in Oxford, Ohio, and surrounding areas revealed that birds in town foraged primarily on the ground, whereas those in nearby forests foraged primarly in the canopy of trees. This ground habitat is often readily available for foraging birds because dense grass lawns are typically the most common vegetative cover in towns like Oxford. Suburban lawns are more productive and provide more food than more natural grassland habitats, and as a result, they are capable of supporting large numbers of birds. In addition, ground-foraging birds probably use less energy walking than those birds that must fly to forage in shrubs or trees. It has also been suggested that birds foraging in open areas, such as those found in towns, are better able to detect and escape from predators. Such advantages may explain why ground-foraging birds like the cardinals are often so common in urban areas.

3

Food and Feeding Habits

Birds have high metabolic rates and use energy at high rates. As a result, birds must eat frequently and must select and digest food efficiently. Cardinals are no exception, and they exhibit several adaptations that enhance their foraging efficiency. Among the most obvious of these adaptations is the bill. Although other groups of animals, such as turtles, have beaklike structures that are superficially similar to the avian bill, the internal design of those structures is quite different. The bird skull and bill represent an elegant compromise between weight and strength.

**NASOFRONTAL
HINGE**

TRABECULAE

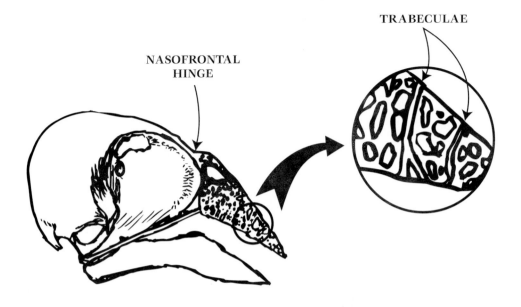

A cross section through a portion of the skull of a cardinal illustrates this compromise. The numerous air spaces (spongy bone) reduce the weight of the skull, and weight reduction was undoubtedly an important factor in the evolution of avian flight. However, also present are numerous bony struts called trabeculae that reinforce the bill and enable it to withstand the substantial forces that result when cardinals bite on and open hard seeds. Notice that the cardinal bill is decurved, which means that it curves sharply downward. Many seed-eating birds have bills with this shape, and this likely represents an adaptation to reduce stress on a potential weak point, the nasofrontal hinge. The forces acting on this point vary with the position of a seed in the bill, and to minimize these forces, cardinals typically hold seeds in the bill below the anterior end of the external nostril. Cardinals can extract seeds from a shell by either crushing or cutting the shell. To crush seeds, a cardinal holds the seed in the bill and presses the seed against the roof of the mouth to eject the seed from the shell. When cutting seeds, a cardinal uses the tongue to hold the seed against the roof of the mouth; then it cuts the shell with rapid forward and backward movements of the cutting edges of the bill. The cut shell is discarded, and the seed is swallowed.

Along with the large bill, cardinals have large jaw muscles. Thus, when cutting or crushing seeds, cardinals can generate a substantial force. One investigator induced cardinals and several other species to bite on a crude measuring device and found that cardinal bills were able to generate more force than those of other seed-eating birds. Thus, cardinals can probably feed on larger seeds, and on a larger variety of seeds, than many other seed-eating birds.

After a cardinal swallows a seed or other food item, it passes through a muscular tube called the esophagus and into the stomach. A bird's stomach has two parts: an anterior portion with a lining that secretes a variety of digestive juices, plus a posterior portion with muscular walls. In birds, this posterior portion, or gizzard, serves as the avian equivalent of teeth and is used to grind and digest hard food items. The gizzard is particularly well developed in seed-eating birds like the cardinal. Once food enters the gizzard, the muscular walls contract and relax, churning and grinding the contents. To enhance the grinding action, the inner lining of the gizzard is covered with a hard, rough surface. The gizzards of seed-eating birds usually contain some sand or grit. One investigator found that about 6 percent of the contents of cardinal stomachs was small quartz fragments and sand. This grit creates more friction in the gizzard and aids in the breakdown and digestion of seeds and other materials.

After being pulverized in the gizzard, food passes into the intestine. Cardinals and other seedeaters typically have longer intestines than do birds that feed primarily on insects or other animals. This is because foods rich in protein (meat or insects) are partially digested by enzymes in the anterior portion of the stomach. Less time is needed, therefore, to complete digestion in the intestine. In contrast, the stomach produces no enzymes that break down the contents of seeds and other plant material (fats and carbohydrates). As a result, food must remain in the intestine for a longer time to complete digestion. Once digested, food is absorbed through the walls of the intestine and distributed by the blood to the rest of the body.

The efficiency with which food is digested and absorbed depends on the type of food eaten. For example, it has been estimated that raptors are able to extract 66 to 88 percent of the energy or calories potentially available in their food. An experiment with cardinals revealed that their digestive efficiency varied with the type of seed ingested. Cardinals were tested with five types of seeds—foxtail, smartweed, hemp, ragweed, and sunflower—and at room temperature (about 77 degrees Fahrenheit), digestive efficiency averaged about 70 percent. However, efficiency ranged from 49 percent for smartweed seeds to 80 percent for sunflower seeds. This variation is probably a result of differences in seed composition, with some simply being easier to digest than others. Digestive efficiency was also

found to vary with temperature, with efficiency an average of 16 percent higher at 77 degrees than at 32 degrees. The reasons for this difference are not clear. However, in an apparent attempt to compensate for this reduced efficiency, cardinals ate nearly two and a half times more food when kept at the lower temperature. These results suggest that free-living cardinals have to consume substantially more food during cold weather, particularly when temperatures drop below freezing. Unfortunately, no experiments have been carried out on free-living cardinals, so it is not clear how much more food they might have to eat.

Although the bill and other parts of the digestive system appear to be specialized for feeding on seeds, cardinals feed on a variety of plants and animals. In 1908, researcher Waldo McAtee examined the contents of 498 cardinal stomachs and found that their diet consisted of about 30 percent animal matter and 70 percent vegetable matter. The animal matter consisted predominantly of insects, including beetles, grasshoppers, crickets, butterfly and moth larvae, cicadas, treehoppers, leafhoppers, and dragonflies, but cardinals occasionally fed on spiders,

centipedes, snails, and slugs. Overall, cardinals fed on at least eighty-five different insects and other invertebrates. Cardinals also fed on at least seventy-seven different plants, with this vegetable matter consisting primarily of seeds of various grains (corn, wheat, oats, sorghum, and rice), wild fruit, and weeds.

Wild fruit seeds, but generally not the pulp, were found in the stomachs of nearly 63 percent of all cardinals. Fruits eaten most frequently included wild grapes, dogwood fruits, black-berries, and raspberries. Weed seeds made up more than half of the vegetable matter eaten by cardinals. Among the seeds eaten were smartweed, bindweed, foxtail and other grasses, sedges, vetch, dock, sow thistle, plantains, chickweed, button weed, and sorrel. Of course, cardinals are fond of sunflower seeds as well. Cardinals have also been observed eating the buds of several species of trees, such as elms and chokecherry, and drinking sap from holes made by Yellow-bellied Sapsuckers.

Cardinals obviously eat a variety of foods, but do they exhibit any preferences? Determining such preferences requires knowledge of availability as well as diet. That is, cardinals may eat certain foods more frequently simply because those foods are more readily available. For example, if someone set up nine feeding stations with corn and one with sunflower seeds and found that 90 percent of the birds' diet was corn, such results would not necessarily indicate a preference for corn, because 90 percent of the available food was corn. A favorite food is one that is eaten more frequently than availability would predict. So if the birds' diet was 90 percent sunflower seeds despite that fact that only 10 percent of the available food was sunflower seeds, that would be evidence of a preference.

Aelred D. Geis, an investigator with the U.S. Fish and Wildlife Service, studied the seed preferences of several species of birds that visit feeding stations. He found that cardinals exhibited the greatest preference for black-striped, gray-striped, and oil-type sunflower seeds and, to a lesser degree, for hulled sunflower seeds and white proso millet. Cardinals ate lesser amounts of buckwheat, cracked corn, milo, hulled oats, peanuts, wheat, and niger seeds and ignored canary seed, flax seed, whole oats, rapeseed, and rice. (See chapter 11 for more details.)

For cardinals foraging away from feeding stations, Waldo McAtee found that corn was eaten more frequently than any other grains. In fact, 7.1 percent of all food eaten by cardinals was corn. Nearly two-thirds of all cardinals sampled had wild fruit in their stomachs, and they usually ate just the seeds rather than the pulp.

Of all fruits, wild grapes were eaten most frequently. McAtee pointed out that there was "no doubt that the redbird feeds upon all kinds of wild grapes growing within its range." The fruits of various dogwoods ranked second to grapes and were eaten by about 10 percent of the 498 cardinals. Among weed seeds, those of the various smartweeds and bindweeds were eaten most frequently, with the seeds of foxtail grasses next in importance. The most frequently eaten insects were beetles of various types, grasshoppers, plus moths and their caterpillars. It is unclear whether cardinals actually prefer these frequently eaten "wild" foods, because no one has examined cardinal food preferences away from feeding stations.

The food habits of cardinals change during the year. More vegetable material is eaten during the colder months of the year, and more animal material is consumed during the warmer months. A study of cardinal food habits over their entire range revealed that more than 75 percent of all food eaten from November through April was vegetable material. In contrast, during July, about 65 percent of their diet was animal material in the form of insects. During the remaining months (May, June, August, September, and October), between 50 and 70 percent of their diet was vegetable material. Such seasonal variation in diet is probably due in part to availability. Throughout the northern parts of their range, insects are available only during the warmer months of the year; as a result, the number of insects in the diet during those months may increase. In the southern and southwestern United States, Mexico, Central America, and Hawaii, cardinals have access to insects throughout most or all of the year and might take more insect prey than do cardinals in the northern United States or Canada.

Factors other than food availability can influence diet. For example, female cardinals might require more calcium in their diets prior to egg laying, because calcium is needed to produce eggshells. Caloric value (energy content) may also be important. In fact, investigators have found that cardinals exposed to colder temperatures tend to prefer seeds that provide the most calories. Additional calories are needed during cold weather because it takes more energy to maintain body temperature. Also, because of the potential benefits of brighter, redder plumage, the diet of male and, to a lesser degree, female cardinals may be influenced by the carotenoid content of available foods prior to and during molt.

The diet of adult cardinals might also be influenced by the need to provide food for young. Cardinal nestlings, like those of many other songbirds, are fed primarily insects and insect larvae, because growing young require lots of protein. So while they are provisioning young, adult cardinals probably spend much of their time searching for insect prey. As a result, adults may increase the amount of insect prey in their own diets.

Yet another factor that influences food selection is a bird's foraging location. Cardinals usually forage either on or close to the ground. A study conducted in North Carolina revealed that foraging cardinals spent 9 percent of their time on bare ground, 23 percent perched in a plant, and 68 percent standing on the ground and feeding from a standing plant. Overall, therefore, foraging cardinals spent 77 percent of their time on the ground. The results of another study, also conducted in North Carolina, indicated that cardinals spent 21 percent of their time on the ground, 67 percent in shrubs, and only 12 percent in the canopy of trees. The results of these two studies suggest that cardinals forage primarily, but not exclusively, on the ground or in low-growing plants or shrubs. As a result, cardinals are more likely to select and eat seeds and insects in those locations.

Cardinals searching for insects, fruits, seeds, and other potential food items rely primarily on their keen vision. Perhaps enhancing this search is the cardinal's ability to see near-ultraviolet (UV) light. Whereas human vision is limited to the visible spectrum (violet through red, or wavelengths between about 380 and 780 nanometers), cardinals and other birds can detect shorter, near-UV wavelengths between 300 and 380 nanometers. This ability may be of great importance to foraging cardinals, because some insects and berries may reflect near-UV light.

4

Vocal Behavior

Taxonomically, Northern Cardinals are members of the avian order Passeriformes, and species in this order are referred to as passerines or songbirds. These species are able to produce vocalizations called songs, which, by definition, are relatively long vocal displays, often with repeated patterns, that are usually pleasing to the human ear and usually play some role in reproduction. Cardinals and other birds also produce other vocalizations referred to as calls, which are relatively short, acoustically simple vocalizations that can serve a variety of functions. Although songs and calls differ in structure and function, they are produced by the same structure, the syrinx.

The syrinx is the avian equivalent of the human larynx, or voice box. The syrinx is unique to birds and is found deep in the chest at the point where the trachea, or windpipe, splits into the two primary bronchi. Birds also have a larynx, but it has no vocal cords and serves only to keep food and water from entering the trachea. The syrinx possesses two thin membranes, called internal tympaniform membranes, that vibrate as air passes by them. Birds, including cardinals, can vary the characteristics of sounds by using syringeal muscles to adjust the tension on these membranes.

Northern Cardinals use the syrinx to produce a variety of calls, with different calls and their variants serving different functions. Among the most frequently uttered calls is the "chip" call ("chip" indicates what the call sounds like). This call is very short in duration (about 0.025 second) and extends over a broad range of frequencies (4,000 to 8,000 hertz, or cycles per second). Many investigators have noted that the chip call has a metallic quality. These calls are given in a variety of contexts and may be given either singly or in a series. When given in a series, the interval between successive chip calls varies, as does the total number of calls in the series. At times, chip calls are repeated slowly; at other times, they are uttered in rapid volleys.

Single chip calls are given by both males and females, and when repeated slowly, they may function as location calls, with members of a pair, a family group, or a flock giving these calls to inform others of their location. In thick vegetation, where maintaining visual contact is difficult if not impossible, such calls may help cardinals stay together.

Adult cardinals, particularly males, sometimes utter chip calls as they slowly approach a nest. These calls may indicate that a nest visit is imminent, permitting the female or nestlings to get ready. If a male is bringing food, such previsit communication allows a faster, more efficient exchange. This could be beneficial, because less time at the nest translates into more time foraging and, perhaps, a reduced likelihood that a predator will be alerted to the presence of the nest.

Chip calls given with increased volume may indicate mild alarm. For example, when a predator is spotted in the territory, cardinals may utter louder and perhaps more frequent chip calls. This informs a mate or fledglings that a potential predator is nearby and increases their chances of avoiding predation. And by varying the volume of chip calls and the rate at which they are uttered, cardinals can provide more precise information. Louder, more frequent calls indicate a greater level of alarm and a greater threat. So, for example, when a predator comes near a nest with young, an adult cardinal may give very loud chip calls at a fast rate.

Chip calls may also signal aggression. They are sometimes given during territorial enounters and, during the nonbreeding period, when two individuals seek access to the same resource, such as a feeding station or other food source. Again, variation in volume and rate of calling may provide information about an individual's level of aggression, with greater volume and faster rates indicating an increased likelihood of interacting.

Another call used by cardinals is the *kwut* or *chuck* call. Like chip calls, kwuts are given by both males and females and are short in duration (also about 0.025 second); however, kwuts are lower in frequency and have a harsher sound (which indicates that the call extends over a wider range of frequencies). Also, kwuts are generally given singly and not in a rapid series. Kwuts signal a high level of arousal or excitement. For example, these calls are given during aggressive encounters at feeding stations or at territorial boundaries, and their use probably indicates that a cardinal is more likely to escalate an encounter. Kwut calls are also given when a potential predator approaches nestlings or fledglings, probably serving to alert a mate and young to the predator's presence.

During particularly intense interactions, male and female cardinals may utter chips and kwuts in rapid alternation, as in *chip-kwut, chip-kwut, chip-kwut*. At times, this call may sound more like *pee-too*. Cardinals may give this call when a rival is very close and an interaction is imminent. For example, this call is sometimes given early in the breeding season when the location of a territory boundary is in dispute or when a trespassing cardinal is being evicted from another's territory.

Much less commonly, adult cardinals use other calls. One such call has been referred to as the "rattle" or "chitter." This is a high-frequency (6,000 to 8,000 hertz) trill consisting of several brief notes uttered in rapid succession. One investigator reported that territorial cardinals gave rattle calls when the songs of other cardinals were played back in their territory with a tape recorder. This response suggests that rattles convey a threat of aggression. However, other investigators reported that cardinals sometimes gave rattle calls after spotting aerial predators such as hawks or falcons, suggesting that this call may also serve to warn other cardinals.

Another call given by adult females is the *see* call. This is a brief (0.2 second), high-frequency (6,000 hertz) call given by females desiring copulation. Successful copulation, during which sperm is transferred into the female reproductive tract, probably requires cooperation by the female, and the *see* call may signal a male to expect such cooperation.

Adult cardinals also shriek or scream when held by a human or when captured and held by a predator. Shrieks are usually about 0.6 to 0.8 second in duration and are given either singly or, more often, in a series. These are very high volume calls with acoustic features that make the caller easy to locate. Similar calls are emitted by many other birds (and by some mammals as well), and there has been much speculation concerning their possible function. It is likely that these calls serve to attract other individuals that may be able to interfere with the threatening predator and allow the caller to escape. Other cardinals rarely respond vigorously to these distress screams, but other predators are sometimes attracted. Thus, it is likely that these screams are meant to attract other, perhaps larger, predators that, in their attempt to take the calling bird from the original predator, may permit the caller to escape. In fact, many studies have revealed that predators, including Sharp-shinned and Cooper's Hawks, are attracted to distress screams. Certainly, the likelihood that a screaming cardinal will escape from a predator is low, but it is not zero. Thus, screaming may be a better strategy than not screaming.

Young cardinals also use several types of calls. Like adults, juveniles utter screams when handled or captured by potential predators. In addition, juveniles utter begging calls. These calls probably help adults monitor the hunger level of their young. At hatching, young cardinals utter high-frequency, low-volume begging calls; with increasing age, these calls become louder and lower in frequency. By the time of fledging, and continuing for several weeks thereafter, the most frequently used call of young cardinals resembles the adult chip call. However, unlike adults, juveniles utter these as a rapid series of two to ten calls. These calls are given, sometimes incessantly, by older fledglings as they follow their parents throughout the territory, and they probably provide adults with information about the hunger level and location of fledglings.

The best-known vocalizations of cardinals are their songs, and in contrast to many species of songbirds, both males and females sing. Typical cardinal songs sound something like *what-cheer, what-cheer, what-cheer* or *purdy, purdy, purdy, whoit, whoit, whoit, whoit.* Although other female songbirds sing, it is usually infrequent. In one study, investigators made detailed observations of 140 female Song Sparrows, and only 12 were ever heard singing. Although female cardinals sing much less than males, many sing regularly during the breeding season, particularly during April and May.

The songs of male and female cardinals are very similar and consist of repetitions of sounds called syllables, with most songs consisting of five to eleven syllables and lasting between 1.5 and 3 seconds. Syllables consist of one, two, or three subunits called notes and are usually about 0.25 second in duration. Most songs are composed of one or two different syllables but on occasion may include three or even four different syllables. Different syllables vary in frequency but are almost always somewhere between 1,300 and 4,500 hertz.

Individual male and female cardinals have repertoires of twelve to eighteen syllables that are used singly or in combination to produce songs. Cardinal songs do not consist of random combinations of syllables. Rather, particular syllables or combinations of syllables are consistently repeated to produce specific song types, and specific song types may be consistently reproduced over many months or even years. When two different syllables are used in a song type, they are almost always used in a particular order, and each syllable is usually repeated several times. For example, if a song consists of syllables A and B, a typical song might be A, A, A, B, B, B, B, B.

Individual male and female cardinals usually have repertoires of eight to twelve of these song types. Song types are not reproduced exactly the same way each time they are used. For example, a song type that consists of several repetitions of the same syllable will exhibit variation in the number of repetitions of that syllable, and a song type consisting of two different syllables will exhibit variation in the number of times each syllable is repeated. However, if two different syllables are used in a particular song type, cardinals rarely, if ever, alter the order in which those syllables appear in the song or use those syllables in combination with other syllables.

Cardinals and most other songbirds sing intermittently. Typically, cardinals utter a series of songs separated by relatively short intervals (usually five to eight seconds between songs) and then cease singing for several minutes. Each series of songs is referred to as a bout, and each bout usually consists of ten to twenty-five songs. However, the number of songs per bout varies, and early in the breeding season, bouts of fifty or sixty songs are not unusual. Occasionally, bouts may consist of more than a hundred songs. During bouts, cardinals generally sing several repetitions of a particular song type. Some bouts consist entirely of one song type, and others consist of two or more song types. During these latter bouts, cardinals may repeat one song type several times, then switch to another song type, which is repeated several times. The pauses between bouts are typically about fifteen to twenty minutes but range from just a minute or two to several hours. Pauses between bouts are typically shorter early in the breeding season.

The acquisition of song by cardinals and other songbirds begins at an early age. At three weeks of age, or even earlier, young cardinals begin producing sounds that are the forerunners of song. These sounds are just low-volume warbles and bear little resemblance to the songs of adults. During their first summer and fall, young cardinals are also listening to the songs of adults. Although unable to reproduce these adult songs, young cardinals memorize some of the syllables and songs for future use. Following the summer and fall learning and listening period, young cardinals enter what is called a silent period. During this period, which extends from late fall through early winter, young cardinals utter various calls but do not attempt to sing.

Beginning in January or February, young cardinals begin to sing. However, singing during this period is low volume and rambling, with little resemblance to typical adult singing. This unstructured singing is commonly referred to as subsong and, unlike adult singing, is not meant to communicate any information. Rather, subsong represents practice. Young cardinals attempt to reproduce syllables or songs being uttered by nearby adults plus those heard the previous summer and fall. There also appears to be some improvisation, with young cardinals sometimes modifying previously heard syllables and, less frequently, creating new ones. During subsong, young cardinals remain low (less than six feet up), often in dense clumps of vegetation. Such locations may be chosen to reduce the chances of being detected by a predator. Although young cardinals are more likely to utter subsong, adults may engage in brief periods of subsong early in the season (January and February) when they are just beginning to sing. As with young cardinals, adults uttering subsong are probably just practicing songs that haven't been uttered for several months.

Subsong may continue for several weeks, and during this time, singing gradually becomes more adultlike. From March through May, song crystallization occurs. Young cardinals decide which songs to include in their repertoires and then practice them until they can be reproduced flawlessly and consistently.

Because young cardinals learning to sing copy the songs of other nearby cardinals, individuals in a particular area often share many, if not all, song types. The extent of this sharing diminishes with increasing distance, and cardinals separated by long distances (several hundred miles) share few, if any, syllables or song types. Thus, cardinals exhibit what ornithologists call dialects. Similar regional variation in the use of syllables or song types has been reported in many other species of songbirds. Local dialects may arise when young males increase their reproductive success by copying the songs of older neighbors. By singing like an older neighbor, young males may improve their chances of obtaining a territory and, later, attracting a mate and raising young. The chances of successfully defending a territory may increase because other males seeking territories may mistakenly believe that an older, more competitive male is present and therefore avoid the young male's territory.

Male cardinals may sing occasionally in January, but sustained singing usually begins in late February or early March and continues into August. It is no coincidence that singing begins as the days become longer. Cardinals, like other birds, have special light receptors in an area of the brain called the hypothalamus. These receptors are stimulated by the longer days of January and February, and in response, the hypothalamus releases hormones that stimulate the pituitary gland. The pituitary then synthesizes and releases hormones that stimulate the testes. The testes of males respond by increasing in size and releasing increasing amounts of the hormone testosterone. Testosterone stimulates growth of those areas in the brain that control singing behavior, and as a result, male cardinals begin to sing.

From January through mid- to late February, male cardinals are more likely to sing on clear days with warm temperatures. Beginning in late February or early March, male singing rates vary with mated status and breeding stage. Males sing at the highest rates (150 to 200 or more songs per hour during the early morning hours) prior to pairing. Singing rates may drop slightly after pairing but tend to remain high while mates are building nests. In contrast, singing rates are lowest (about 50 to 75 songs per hour) when males are feeding nestlings and recently fledged young. Singing rates are intermediate (about 75 to 150 songs per hour) during incubation and when males are caring for fledged young and their mates are constructing new nests.

Male cardinals also exhibit daily variation in singing rates. As in many other species of songbirds, the males engage in a dawn chorus, with singing typically beginning half an hour or more before sunrise and continuing until shortly after sunrise. Another increase in singing rates typically occurs as sunset approaches. The extent of singing at other times of the day varies with breeding stage. Prior to pairing and while mates are nest building, male cardinals sing intermittently throughout the day. During other breeding stages, males sing very little, if at all, during late morning and through the afternoon. Males may sing primarily at dawn and dusk because atmospheric conditions are generally more favorable (for example, there may be less wind) and light levels may be too low to engage in other activities, such as foraging.

When singing, male cardinals prefer high, exposed locations, because such locations make it easier to observe potential predators and any nearby cardinals (potential mates or territorial intruders), and they also maximize sound transmission. Early in the year (January through March, and into April in more northern locations), there is little vegetation, and males have numerous singing perches to choose from. However, after leaf-out and as vines and other vegetation develop, some perches, such as those within the crowns of large trees, are used less frequently.

Males then use more exposed perches, such as dead branches, the very tops of tall trees, or, in more developed areas, utility wires or antennas. Males often have favorite singing perches in their territories and rarely use other perches.

It has long been recognized that bird song may be important in establishing territories and attracting mates. However, recent studies of a variety of species reveal that singing can also serve a number of other functions. For example, song may be used to solicit extra-pair copulations, coordinate activities around the nest, inform an incubating or brooding mate of the presence or absence of potential predators, stimulate the reproductive activity of mates, help maintain contact with a mate or offspring, and distract potential predators. The singing of male cardinals probably serves many, if not all, of these functions.

Male cardinals must engage in interactions with other males as they establish and maintain territorial boundaries, and song plays an important role in such interactions. Particularly during the period of territory establishment, neighboring males often engage in countersinging. When countersinging, males in adjacent territories sing at the same time, sometimes giving songs alternately and sometimes simultaneously. Males may alter their singing in several ways to convey information. For example, when countersinging, male cardinals sometimes switch song types and begin to sing the same song type being used by the other male. This is referred to as matching, and such behavior probably informs the male being matched that the singing is directed specifically at him. The message conveyed by matching is simply "stay off my territory." Male cardinals can increase the intensity of this message by singing longer songs with a greater number of syllables and by ending songs with a harsh trill. Observations indicate that these trills are added to songs when other males approach too closely. Longer songs and the addition of the trill probably signal an increased likelihood of interacting and warn other males that they may be chased or even attacked if they approach any closer.

Female cardinals sing at much lower rates than males and primarily before nesting begins. Later in the season, when incubating eggs or brooding young, females occasionally sing from the nest. When singing during the prenesting period, female cardinals are usually accompanied by males, either mates or potential mates, and such accompanied bouts of song are referred to as duets.

Duetting prior to nesting may permit paired cardinals to become familiar with, and learn, the song types of their mates. In support of this idea, male and female cardinals sometimes match song types during duets. Such matching could also represent an investment of time and energy important in establishing and maintaining a pair-bond. That is, if there are benefits to knowing each other's song repertoires, then a pair that has expended the time and effort to learn each other's songs may be more likely to stay together.

Paired cardinals may sing from or near nests during the incubation and nestling periods, and it has been suggested that a female cardinal on a nest may match her singing mate's song type to inform him that he need not bring food to the nest. Such communication is beneficial, because it limits unnecessary visits to the nest by the more colorful and conspicuous male, perhaps reducing the chances that a predator will locate the nest. Some predators might use the female's songs to locate a nest, but snakes, which are among the most common predators of cardinal eggs and nestlings, may be more likely to use movement to locate nests.

Many songbirds, including cardinals, have repertoires of different song types. A number of factors have probably contributed to the evolution of song type repertoires in male and female cardinals. For example, having a repertoire of song types increases the likelihood that at least some song types will be shared with neighbors and mates. Such sharing permits matching, which may permit more precise communication. It is also possible, although not clearly demonstrated for cardinals, that different song types in a repertoire may convey different information. Among some warblers, for example, one song type is used during interactions with males and another is used during interactions with females. More study of cardinal singing behavior is needed before any conclusions can be drawn, but it is possible that certain song types signal certain tendencies; that is, certain song types may signal an increased likelihood of aggression, and others may convey the opposite.

Another factor favoring larger song type repertoires is that they may be more effective in stimulating a mate than single song types. For example, a study of canaries revealed that females exposed to larger repertoires of song types built nests at a faster rate and laid more eggs than females exposed to smaller repertoires. Although there is currently no experimental evidence, it is possible that larger repertoires may have a similar effect on female cardinals.

5

Behavior

Locomotion

Birds that occupy wooded, brushy habitats face the problem of trying to fly through areas with lots of branches and leaves. Although providing a little less lift, shorter wings are favored in such habitats because they improve maneuverability and make it easier for birds to avoid all the potential obstacles. Northern Cardinals are typically found in areas with lots of shrubs and trees, so, not surprisingly, they have wings with a relatively low aspect ratio— the ratio of wing length to width. These wings serve cardinals well, because most of their flights cover relatively short distances and are often through relatively dense vegetation.

As with wings, the legs and feet of birds vary with habitat and lifestyle. Northern Cardinals spend most of their time perched in shrubs or trees and occasionally come to the ground to forage, drink, or bathe. As a result, cardinals have feet typical of perching birds—three toes projecting forward, one projecting backward, and each toe with a curved nail for effectively gripping small branches. When cardinals move about on the ground, they hop rather than walk.

Self-maintenance

Feathers serve many functions. They provide the streamlining needed for flight, and wing feathers provide both lift and propulsion. Feathers also protect a bird's skin and can play an important role in the maintenance of body temperature. Feather color often provides information about a bird's species, sex, and age. Feathers may also provide camouflage. For a cardinal's feathers to serve these and other functions, they must be kept in good condition. Once fully developed, feathers are dead structures with no internal system of nourishment or maintenance. Cardinals keep their feathers in good condition by preening, during which they use their bills to apply secretions from the uropygial or preen gland. These oily secretions contain a mixture of waxes, fatty acids, fat, and water and help preserve feather moistness and flexibility and may also protect feathers from bacteria and fungi. Preening cardinals may also be removing feather parasites.

Bathing also helps cardinals keep their feathers in good condition. When bathing, cardinals and many other birds typically immerse the head, raise it, then beat their wings. Bathing removes dust and dirt from feathers and may also help remove feather parasites.

Cardinals have also been observed sunbathing. When sunbathing, birds fluff their feathers, spread their tail feathers, and either droop or extend one or both wings. Birds sunbathe on cold days to acquire heat from the solar radiation. However, cardinals also sunbathe on very warm days, and recent evidence suggests that the resulting high temperatures cause increased activity by feather parasites, making it easier for a preening bird to remove them.

Infrequently, cardinals also engage in an activity referred to as anting. Anting has been observed in over 200 species of birds and may be either passive or active. In passive anting, a bird simply sits on an anthill and allows ants to move among its ruffled feathers. In active anting, a bird picks up ants with its bill and releases them somewhere in its plumage. The function of anting remains unclear, but it is possible that the introduced ants eat or repel feather parasites. It has also been suggested that the ants secrete chemicals that inhibit the growth of bacteria and fungi. As ants move through and among feathers, these secretions are picked up by a bird's feathers and skin and may reduce the likelihood of bacterial or fungal infections.

Roosting and Sleeping

Northern cardinals spend a good portion of their lives roosting, but, unfortunately, little is known about this activity. Observations suggest that, particularly during the nonbreeding season, cardinals spend a substantial portion of the daylight hours roosting low in thick, dense shrubs or thickets. Dense conifers, such as eastern red cedars, are also commonly used as roost sites. Cardinals roosting for extended periods may spend some of their time sleeping, but it is likely that roosting cardinals are usually awake but inactive. Such inactivity is doubly beneficial. First, energy is conserved by limiting movement and by selecting a roost site sheltered from the elements. Second, assuming that the roost site is well hidden, a roosting cardinal is less likely to be spotted by a predator than is an active, mobile cardinal.

Sites selected for nocturnal roosting and sleeping are similar to those selected for daylight roosting: low in dense shrubs or thickets or dense conifers. Unlike some species, cardinals

apparently do not share their nocturnal roost sites. However, during the breeding season, females typically spend the night on the nest, and after fledging, the nocturnal roosts of siblings may be close together, although not necessarily in the same shrub or tree. At nocturnal roosts, cardinals spend some time sleeping, but they are probably awake much of the time, especially during the warmer months of the year. Spending as much time awake as is physiologically possible may reduce the likelihood of being captured by a nocturnal predator.

Nonvocal Communication

Communication is a process in which individuals use specially designed signals or displays to transmit information to other individuals. Many avian signals are vocal, but birds, including cardinals, also use a variety of visual displays. Some of these displays are used by cardinals primarily during courtship, and others are used in aggressive contexts. One cardinal display is referred to as the asymmetrical or lopsided display. During this display, typically given by males in the presence of females, a cardinal twists its body to expose its belly and the underside of its partially spread tail. During the display, the beak is closed, the crest is lowered, the feathers of the neck and body are sleeked back, and the wings may be lifted away from the body. This display appears to have both sexual and aggressive elements, perhaps revealing conflicting desires to approach for sexual purposes and to attack to prevent another individual from coming too close. The conflict signaled by the lopsided display is further revealed by its similarities to two other displays—a courtship display called the song-dance display and an aggressive display called the head-forward display.

During the song-dance display, male cardinals assume a posture similar to that in the lopsided display but remain more upright, erect the crest, and sing. During this display, males sway to and fro in front of a female. Males giving this display may be seeking to pair or copulate with a female.

The head-forward display (shown here) is clearly aggressive and is used by both males and females in the presence of another nearby bird. This display is given by males while feeding during the winter and by both sexes while defending their territory during the breeding season. During this display, a cardinal faces its opponent with body held low, crest lowered, and mouth open. Cardinals giving this display may also spread and vibrate their wings.

A cardinal confronted with the head-forward display may respond with a submission display. During this display, cardinals usually raise the crest, fluff the feathers of the upper breast, crouch slightly with the neck pulled back, point the bill slightly upward, and avoid looking at the other. The submission display signals a desire to avoid conflict, and to ensure that outcome, the submissive bird may fly away.

During an aggressive encounter between two equally matched cardinals, it is possible that neither individual will exhibit submission, and the encounter may escalate. One cardinal flies directly at the other, with the aggressor trying to supplant or usurp the perch of the other cardinal. Such supplanting attacks may occur several times. The supplanted individual may fly away, with the aggressor following and chasing. Sometimes, however, the attacked individual doesn't flee but instead flies up toward the attacker at the last moment. Both birds then flutter in the air while grappling with their feet. Usually fighting stops immediately after such an encounter, and one or both cardinals retreat from the scene of the fight. Occasionally, the fighting continues and both birds fall to the ground while attempting to peck or bite each other. Rarely do such encounters last more than a few seconds, and even more rarely do such encounters result in injuries to the combatants. Such aggression is most likely to occur between males during the period of territory establishment, but it may also occur during the winter as males fight for feeding sites, such as bird feeders. Although not as common, female cardinals sometimes respond aggressively to other females, particularly during the period of territory establishment and pair formation. Paired females are particularly aggressive at this time, because unpaired females may be seeking to pair with their mates.

During the period of territory establishment, male and, less frequently, female cardinals occasionally see reflections of themselves in windows or mirrors. What follows, as far as a cardinal is concerned, is an interaction with an opponent that cannot be intimidated and will not flee. As a result, a cardinal may repeatedly attack and attempt to grapple with his or her opponent. Territorial birds sometimes continue such attacks of their mirror images for extended periods and may injure themselves or make themselves vulnerable to predation. Covering the mirror or window makes the apparently fearless opponent disappear and puts an end to the fighting.

During courtship, male cardinals sometimes give a song-flight display. During this display, a male fluffs out his breast feathers, raises the crest, spreads the tail, and flies toward and usually lands near a female. As he slowly flies toward the female, the male holds his body erect and his head upright, beats his wings using short, rapid strokes, and usually sings. Song-flights may be as short as a few feet and as long as one hundred feet. These displays are given primarily early in the breeding season and probably play a role in pair formation. Males and females apparently do not copulate after male song-flight displays, indicating that the display is not used to solicit copulation.

Courtship feeding has been observed in many species of songbirds, including Northern Cardinals, and this behavior typically occurs during pair formation. During courtship feeding, female cardinals assume a posture similar to that of begging fledglings and quiver their wings. Males respond to this display by approaching the female with food. During the early stages of pair formation, male cardinals provide food only when solicited in this manner by females. Later, however, males may present food to their mates without such solicitation. The rate of courtship feeding, or perhaps the quality of food delivered by males, may provide females with important information about male quality. If so, courtship feeding is important in helping female cardinals choose their mates.

Female cardinals indicate their readiness to copulate by giving a precopulatory display. During this display, females fluff their breast feathers, quiver their wings, and point the beak and tail upward. With the tail up, the cloacal opening, where sperm are introduced by the male, is exposed. Females may also give low-volume, high-frequency calls during this display.

Spacing

Northern Cardinals defend what ornithologists call all-purpose territories— territories in which all important activities take place, including mating, nesting, and feeding. These territories are defended only during the breeding season, generally beginning sometime in February or March and extending through August or September. The size of these territories varies with habitat quality and population density but generally ranges from about 0.8 to 4 hectares (about 2 to 10 acres). Near the northern edge of their range (e.g., southern Canada), cardinals are less abundant, and territories may be as large as 23 hectares (about 58 acres). Territories are defended primarily by males.

With the breakup of winter flocks in February or March, male cardinals begin to sing, and chases among males become more frequent. During this time, males gradually range over smaller areas and begin to defend these areas with increasing vigor. Territories are established by singing as well as through displays, chases, and fights. Older males may establish territories in the same area year after year, and their territories are typically established before those of first-year males. In areas with high densities of males, territory boundaries may be very well defined. With decreasing densities, boundaries may become less precise. Boundaries may also fluctuate during the breeding season. One factor contributing to such fluctuation may be the location of the nest. During nesting, male activity is centered around the nest, and as a result, boundaries some distance away may not be defended as vigorously. Neighboring males may then extend their territories into these less well defended areas. Female cardinals do not defend territories as vigorously as males, but they will chase intruding females from their territories, especially if such intruding females come near a territorial female's mate or nest. The vigor of defense declines somewhat during the breeding season as cardinals direct their attention and efforts to other activities, such as feeding nestlings or fledglings.

Although cardinals spend most of their time in their territories, they occasionally trespass into nearby territories to gain access to particular resources (food or water), to determine the nesting status of neighboring individuals, and, in a related vein, to seek partners for extra-pair copulations.

As the breeding season ends, generally in September or early October, the intensity of territory defense declines, and trespassing by other cardinals occurs more frequently. By mid- to late October, territory boundaries are no longer defended, and males, as well as females and juveniles, may move into areas well beyond their former territories.

6

The Breeding Season:
Phenology, Courtship, and Nesting Success

The range of Northern Cardinals extends over a broad area, and throughout most of this range, the timing of breeding exhibits little variation. In most areas, the breeding season extends from February through September. During February, March, and early April, male cardinals sing to establish territories and attract mates. Actual nesting usually begins sometime between early April and mid-May and ends sometime between mid-July and early September. Female cardinals first start to build nests in mid- to late April in areas ranging from as far south as Arizona to as far north as Ontario. The nesting season may end a bit sooner for cardinals at the northern edge of their range. For example, cardinals in Ontario rarely begin new nests after mid- to late August, whereas birds in New York or Michigan and farther south may continue to initiate new nests as late as early September. Northern Cardinals

introduced into Hawaii breed throughout the year. Although little information is available, it is also likely that Northern Cardinals at the southern edge of their range (southern Mexico and northern Central America) breed on a different schedule than their northern counterparts.

45

Within populations, studies of other species indicate that age is one factor that influences the timing of reproduction. Typically, older individuals begin breeding before younger individuals, particularly first-time breeders. Several factors may contribute to the later initiation of breeding by first-year birds. First, young males must establish territories, and they are usually at a competitive disadvantage. Older male cardinals often remain in or near their territories from previous years, so as the breeding season begins, they can quickly reestablish dominance in their old territories. Younger males may have to move around looking for open territories; as a result, they often establish territories later than the older, established males. Similarly, older cardinals often form pairs before first-year birds because they pair up with their mates from the previous year, and re-forming a pair-bond takes less time than forming a new one. A third factor might be differences in physical condition. Some studies suggest that older birds forage more efficiently than first-year birds. They have more foraging experience and are better at locating food. As a result, older birds may be in better physical condition and have larger energy reserves than younger birds. Because many reproductive activities (for example, defending a territory or producing a clutch of eggs) require the expenditure of substantial amounts of energy, older birds can start breeding before younger birds. Starting earlier is generally advantageous, because studies of a number of species have revealed that earlier breeders are more successful; they produce more young, and the young are more likely to survive. One reason for this increased survival is that young from earlier broods are older and have more time to develop their skills, including foraging skills, than young from later broods. These older, perhaps larger, juveniles are usually able to dominate smaller, less experienced young from later nests and are therefore more likely to survive.

During the nesting season, cardinal pairs may attempt to raise three, four, or even five broods. At best, however, only one or two of these nesting attempts are likely to be successful, and rarely are more than four broods raised during one breeding season. Studies conducted throughout their range indicate that, typically, only 15 to 30 percent of all nests are successful. Predation of eggs or nestlings is the primary cause of nest failure. However, some cardinal nests fail as a result of Brown-headed or Bronzed Cowbird parasitism or natural causes, such as being dislodged by the growth of nest-support vegetation or by wind.

After a nest fails, female cardinals quickly begin building a new nest in a new location. The interval between loss of a nest and the initiation of another clutch may be as short as four days but more typically is five to seven days. This interval is usually somewhat longer in April and May, probably because cold weather inhibits ovulation.

An array of predators are responsible for the failure of cardinal nests. Because nest predation is rarely observed, probable predators are usually identified based on the appearance of predated nests. When a predated nest is torn apart or pulled from its original position, the likely predator is a larger mammal. Among the large mammals that sometimes eat cardinal eggs and nestlings are raccoons, striped skunks, spotted skunks, opossums, coyotes, gray foxes, and red foxes. Predated nests showing no signs of disturbance have probably been lost to birds, snakes, or small mammals. Among the birds most likely to prey on cardinal nests are Blue Jays and American Crows. Snakes thought to prey on cardinal nests include rat snakes, milk snakes, black racers, corn snakes, eastern coachwhips, and garter snakes. Small mammals that prey on cardinal eggs and nestlings include eastern chipmunks, white-footed mice, fox squirrels, and least weasels. Most studies suggest that the primary predators of cardinal nests are snakes and small mammals.

Birds exhibit a diversity of mating systems. Most species, however, including Northern Cardinals, are monogamous. In monogamous species, individuals form prolonged pair-bonds with one member of the opposite sex. Male and female cardinals typically form pair-bonds that last for an entire breeding season. However, pair-bonds may be briefer, lasting for just one breeding attempt, or longer, extending over two or more breeding seasons.

Most male and female cardinals appear to form pair-bonds from February through early April. Males and females paired to each other during previous breeding seasons are often the first to pair up as a new breeding season approaches, sometimes forming pairs as early as January. During February and into March, males and females may seem to be associating with each other, but these early associations do not always result in pairing. For example, one investigator reported that a male cardinal associated with four different females on his territory during February and March before finally forming a pair-bond. As males begin to establish territories, females temporarily associate with them, perhaps to examine the quality of a male, his territory, or both. If a female finds the male or his territory lacking, she may move to another male's territory or, if there is a period of inclement weather, perhaps rejoin a flock.

The formation of a pair-bond begins with a male cardinal establishing a territory. Males sing at high rates prior to pair formation, and one likely function of this singing is to attract the attention of females. Females entering a male's territory may spend some time feeding and resting but eventually approach the male's position. A male spotting a female in his territory may respond with a song-flight display. Females may fly as the male approaches and, if so, the male typically flies after her. Such chases, after song-flight displays and at other times, may occur frequently during the first few days after a

pair's initial encounter. A female attempting to perch after a chase is likely to be supplanted and chased again. By remaining in a male's territory despite frequent chasing and supplanting, a female may be indicating her willingness to pair. Male cardinals descending toward females during a song-flight may be advertising their physical condition and perhaps the condition and quality of their plumage. During these flights, males fly with wings and tail spread, apparently giving females a good look at the plumage in these areas. The persistence of male cardinals as they chase potential mates early in the pairing process may provide females with additional information about their physical condition.

During courtship, male and female cardinals also duet. During duets, males and females often countersing, with one singing a song and then the other. At other times, their songs overlap. Even though male and female cardinals possess repertoires of several different song types, during duets, males and females often sing the same song type—in other words, they match song types. Male cardinals are more likely to initiate duets than are females, and a male may sing several songs before the female joins in. Also, males usually utter more songs during duets than females do. Early in the pairing process, a cardinal (male or female) choosing to participate in a duet with another individual may be indicating a willingness to at least consider pairing. This early duetting may also provide information about the quality of a potential mate. It has been demonstrated in some species, for example, that older, and therefore better-quality, individuals have larger song-type repertoires than first-year birds. During a series of duets, participants may be able to determine the size of their potential mate's repertoire and gain some information about his or her quality.

After pairing, duetting serves somewhat different functions. A female sings with her mate to advertise her presence and, simultaneously, the mated status of her mate. Such behavior is important for mate retention, because other females in the area may still be looking for mates. Although this advertising may reduce the chance of another female entering a female's territory seeking a mate, some trespassing is likely to occur. In response, mated females attempt to drive female trespassers from their territory. These interactions involve vigorous chasing and, less commonly, physical contact and fighting.

During courtship, cardinals also engage in courtship feeding. Such feeding may provide females with information about the foraging abilities of males, with efficient foragers being able to provide more and perhaps better-quality food. A male's foraging ability is probably an important consideration in mate selection, because later in the season, males must be able to provide food for incubating and brooding females plus nestlings. The prey presented by males to females may also provide females with information about the quality of a male's territory, because males with better-quality territories should be able to provide females with more and better-quality food.

In addition to providing information about male and territory quality,

courtship feeding may also help females prepare for egg laying. Producing a clutch of eggs requires a substantial energy investment by females. The food obtained by females in courtship feeding provides energy and, at the same time, permits females to spend less time foraging themselves. By spending less time in active foraging, female cardinals are able to direct more of their available energy to egg production.

Variation in the rate of courtship feeding by male cardinals indicates that the food provided to females could be important in egg production. Prior to nesting, males feed females about once every four or five minutes. However, when females are constructing nests and laying eggs, male cardinals feed their mates at much higher rates, sometimes as frequently as once a minute or more. The food provided by males represents a substantial contribution of energy and may enable female cardinals to produce larger clutches.

7

Nest Building, Egg Laying, and Incubation

Between pair formation and the beginning of nest construction, female cardinals visit several potential nest sites. These sites are generally along the edges of wooded areas or in thick clumps of vegetation in more open areas, and in shrubs, fencerows, and hedges in urban or suburban areas. When a female visits a potential nest site, she may fluff her feathers and turn her body, perhaps to determine whether the site is large enough and provides sufficient cover. Between visits to different sites, females engage in other activities such as feeding and preening. For the first nest of the year, actual nest building usually begins a few days after a site is visited. Site selection for nests built later in the breeding season takes much less time. After a nest has been lost to predation, female cardinals may begin construction of a new nest within twenty-four hours. Female cardinals appear to be primarily responsible for choosing nest sites. However, males often accompany their mates during the selection process and may have some influence on the female's decision.

Cardinals build nests in many different trees and shrubs. A study in Michigan revealed that cardinals built nests in fifty-three different species of trees, shrubs, and vines, and a study in Indiana revealed that cardinals used eleven species for nesting. Cardinals apparently look for sites that offer protection and concealment, and many species of plants meet these requirements, particularly later in the breeding season. Finding such sites early in the season may be more difficult. In many parts of their range, female cardinals frequently choose sites in eastern red cedars for their first nests (in April or early May), probably because cedars provide cover at a time when deciduous trees and shrubs do not.

Although nests are constructed primarily by females, males sometimes assist by bringing nest material or, less frequently, by helping with the actual construction. As females gather nest material, they are often accompanied by their mates. A male's proximity to his mate may serve at least two functions. First, females may be more vulnerable to predation when preoccupied by nest construction, and males can alert their mates to the presence of potential predators. Second, females are probably fertile during nest construction, and their nearby mates

may be able to reduce the chances of their copulating with other males. Cardinals usually build nests about four to seven feet above the ground. Although nests can range anywhere from two to forty feet above the ground, nests above twenty feet are rare. Nest location tends to change as the breeding season progresses, with cardinals building nests higher later in the season. In addition, cardinals tend to build nests proportionately higher in plants as the breeding season progresses. Cardinals usually place nests about 60 percent of the distance up the plant (for example, a nest in a ten-foot tree would be about six feet up), but later in the breeding season, nests are relatively higher. One possible reason for this difference is that the growing vegetation obstructs vision and movement in low nests. Thus, cardinals in a low nest might be less likely to detect an approaching predator and, once detected, would have fewer escape routes. In addition, as vines and other plants grow higher, more cover is provided, which might also contribute to the increase in nest height later in the season.

As nest building begins, female cardinals first construct a platform using stiff weed stems that are one-sixteenth of an inch or less in diameter. These stems are usually about five or six inches long but may range anywhere from half an inch to about ten inches long, and females break them off while perching on a branch or on the ground. Often, females carry four or five at a time to the nest site and then use their bills to trim any branches off the main stems. The platform is usually started on a cluster of small branches and stems in the nest tree or shrub. While sitting on the platform, a female may grasp the stems and twigs in her bill to bend them. Long stems and twigs may be bent in several places so that they wrap around her body. As the female works, she turns around in the nest and presses outward with her body to ensure that the nest assumes the appropriate shape. Occasionally, females appear to jump up and down on loose material to force it into place.

After completion of the platform, females add a cup-shaped layer of dead leaves occasionally intertwined with ribbons of fine bark, such as the bark of grapevines. An investigator in Indiana found that females preferred the leaves of sugar maples and American beeches, because they were relatively smooth. Because paper and plastic are also smooth, female cardinals in urban areas may incorporate these materials into the "leaf layer." The smooth surface of the leaves makes it easier for the female to rotate its body on this layer as subsequent layers of the nest are added.

After placing leaves on the nest platform, females sit on the leaves to press them into the platform. Then they lean forward and press against the leaves while treading backward with their feet. These movements are accompanied by frequent side-to-side rocking movements. The result of such movements is the formation of a cup-shaped depression.

Next comes a layer that consists of either bark stripped from grapevines or, if grapevines are not available, fine weed stems that are one-thirty-second of an inch or less in diameter. Some females incorporate both bark and stems into this layer. Finally, the lining of the nest consists of very fine (one-sixty-fourth of an inch or less in diameter) rootlets, grass stems, or weed stems. Females collect this material by grasping the base of dry grass or weed plants with their bills and then pulling upward. After placing the material on the nest, females sit on it and press down with a rocking motion.

Most nest construction occurs between 7:30 and 11:30 A.M., but some work, especially for nests built later in the season, may be performed at other times of the day. Construction of a nest usually takes three to six days but can take as long as nine days. Part of this variation may be the result of weather conditions. For example, light rain slows down the rate of construction, and construction stops completely during heavy rain. Very high and very low temperatures can also slow down construction. The first nest of the season generally takes longer to build than nests later in the season.

Occasionally, females begin constructing a nest but fail to complete it. The reasons for this are often unclear, but females may decide that the site will not provide sufficient support or protective cover. The presence of a potential predator near an incomplete nest may also cause abandonment. If a predator spots an incomplete nest, it may return later when eggs or young are present, so a female may improve her chances of successfully raising young by abandoning the site and starting a new nest elsewhere.

Completed nests typically have an outside diameter of 4 to 5 inches, an inner diameter of 2.5 to 3.5 inches, a total height of 2 to 3 inches, and an inner depth of 1.5 to 2 inches. One investigator examined a cardinal nest in great detail and found that the platform consisted of thirty-two pieces of fine, stiff weed stems, most of which were 7 to 10 inches in length. Next came a layer with twelve leaves plus sixteen strips of bark that were about three-eighths of an inch wide and 5 to 10 inches long. The next layer consisted of sixty-nine weed stems (mainly 7 to 12 inches long) plus thirty fine pieces of vine. Finally, the lining of the nest consisted of a compact layer of numerous small sections of grass stems.

Cardinal nests are containers for eggs and, later, nestlings, and they serve a variety of functions. One important function is to provide a suitable microclimate for the eggs, the nestlings, and the incubating or brooding adult. A microclimate consists of the environmental conditions in a very small area, such as a nest, and one of the most important components of a nest microclimate is the temperature. The nest temperature must be different from the surrounding temperature, because eggs and young nestlings require just the right amount of warmth. In addition, a nest's ability to retain heat can have a substantial impact on the energy that an incubating or brooding adult must expend.

The warmth of a cardinal nest is influenced by location and structure. For example, a nest located in an area sheltered from the wind or a nest with leaves and branches over it (that is, a "roof") may be better at retaining heat. Leaves and branches over a nest may also provide shade that can help prevent temperatures from getting too high. Among the important structural characteristics of a nest are its thickness and density—the concentration of stems, twigs, and other nest components. Thick, dense walls provide good insulation that helps maintain the appropriate microclimate. The importance of such insulation is illustrated by the variation in the structure of cardinal nests during the breeding season. Cardinal nests tend to be heavier and thicker early in the breeding season, perhaps because temperatures are typically lower and there is a greater need for insulation.

Cardinals, like many other birds that build open-cup nests, suffer high rates of nest predation. As a result, female cardinals might be expected to build nests in locations that provide the greatest likelihood of nesting success. Surprisingly, however, recent studies suggest that nest site location has little to do with the probability of predation. For example, investigators found no correlation between the degree of nest concealment and the proportion of successful nests. Similarly, no differences were found in the predation rates on accessible versus inaccessible nests (nests located over water, in thorny vegetation, or at the end of thin branches or twigs). Nest height (distance above ground) also had no effect on predation rates. Indeed, there appears to be no single factor or combination of factors that can accurately predict the chance of nest success. Perhaps as a result of this absence of significant factors, cardinals build nests in a variety of different plant species and in a variety of locations in those plants.

Cardinals do not, however, build their nests just anywhere. Rather, female cardinals seem to follow several simple rules when choosing a nest site: provide some concealment for the nest, build within a few feet of the ground, build the sides of the nest higher as the season progresses, and build the nest relatively higher in plants as the season progresses. These rules could very well be an evolutionary response to enhance the probability of selecting a safe nest site. However, in areas with lots of different predators, such rules appear to be of limited value. Predators use different methods when searching for nests, so a site that is safe from one type of predator may be vulnerable to another. For example, a low nest site may be less vulnerable to avian predators such as Blue Jays and American Crows but more vulnerable to ground-based predators such as chipmunks and snakes. So, rather than following complex rules in an attempt to place nests in nonexistent safe sites, the best strategy for cardinals is to use simple rules and renest as rapidly as possible after a nest is lost to predation.

Cardinal nesting success varies with location, with higher success rates in human-dominated habitats, such as small towns or suburban areas, than in more rural areas. Such differences occur because human-dominated habitats probably have reduced populations of nest predators such as snakes. Several studies also revealed that cardinal nesting success improves as the breeding season progresses, and similar improvement has been reported in several other species. Several factors might contribute to this improvement. For example, investigators studying Wood Thrushes suggested that nesting success increased because foliage became denser and provided more cover as the summer progressed. This seems unlikely to be true for cardinals, however, because there appears to be no relationship between degree of nest concealment and nesting success. A second factor that could explain the improved nesting success later in the season is a reduction in clutch and brood sizes. Female cardinals, and females in many other passerine species, typically produce smaller clutches later in the breeding season. Whereas a first nest of the year might have four or five eggs, later nests usually have only two or three.

Assuming that adults put about the same effort into all nests, each nestling in these later nests receives better care (for example, more food) and may be more likely to survive. Currently, there is little evidence to support this idea. Another possible, and perhaps the most likely, explanation is reduced predation pressure. Some investigators found that some snakes, such as racers and rat snakes, become less active, and eat less, during the hot summer months and, as a result, destroy fewer nests.

Female cardinals are fertile from about the time they start building nests until the day that the next to last egg is laid. In other words, any sperm deposited in the female reproductive tract during this period could fertilize an egg. Although sperm usually comes from a female's mate, this is not always the case. The mating system of Northern Cardinals is best described as monogamous, a system in which one male and one female typically remain together throughout a breeding season and cooperate in raising young. In practice, however, the mating system of cardinals and many other "monogamous" species is a bit more complicated. There is now evidence that individuals in many monogamous species utilize what is called a mixed mating strategy. This strategy involves forming a pair-bond with one individual but pursuing copulations with other individuals. At least some male cardinals, and probably some females, use this strategy. So although cardinals are socially monogamous, forming a pair-bond with just one member of the opposite sex, they are not always genetically monogamous, because males and females may copulate with individuals other than their social mates. As a result, nests may contain eggs and young of mixed parentage. For example, three young cardinals in a particular nest may not have the same genetic father, or they may have the same genetic father, but that genetic father may not be their social father (the male paired with their mother). Young fathered by a male other than the social father are typically referred to as extra-pair young, because they result from extra-pair copulations (copulations between individuals that are not pair-bonded). A recent study conducted in Kentucky revealed that three of nineteen nests (15.8 percent) contained such extra-pair young. These nineteen nests contained thirty-seven nestlings, five of which (13.5 percent) were extra-pair young.

Extra-pair young were identified by comparing portions of their DNA with that of their presumed parents. Young birds receive half of their genetic material from their mother and half from their father. If, as was found in the Kentucky study, analysis reveals that a young cardinal shares less genetic material with its social father than with its social mother, and that the young cardinal has genetic material not found in either of

its social parents, then it is apparent that the social father is not the genetic father.

What is not apparent from this type of analysis is whether the female cardinal actively pursued the extra-pair copulation or whether a male forced the female to participate. Observations of cardinals suggest that at least some males actively pursue extra-pair

copulations by trespassing into territories where there are fertile females. Less frequently, females also trespass into neighboring territories. Such behavior suggests that some females may actively pursue extra-pair copulations. Observations also indicate that male cardinals are rarely able (for reasons discussed later) to successfully copulate with females—that is, successfully transfer sperm—unless the female cooperates. Because some extra-pair copulations are obviously successful, such observations further support the conclusion that some female cardinals are willing participants.

As in other species of birds, male cardinals benefit from extra-pair behavior by increasing their reproductive success at the expense of other males. Extra-pair young may be particularly valuable for some male cardinals because of the high rates of predation. As already pointed out, most cardinal nesting attempts produce no young. So by fathering young in more than one nest, males may increase their chances of successful reproduction.

The most likely benefits for female cardinals include fertility insurance and greater genetic quality of young. Little is known about male infertility in wild birds generally or in Northern Cardinals specifically. However, it does occur, and there is evidence that the number of sperm per ejaculate varies among different males of the same species. It is possible, therefore, that female cardinals improve their chances of producing fertile eggs by obtaining sperm from more than one male.

The other possible benefit might be improved genetic quality of offspring. That is, females engaging in extra-pair copulations with males of better quality than their mates will produce better-quality young (that is, young with "good genes"). These good genes could produce what biologists call "sexy sons." In other words, these good genes could produce sons with characteristics that are attractive to females. Being "attractive," these males might attract better-quality mates and/or more extra-pair partners and, as a result, might produce more offspring (more "grandchildren" for their mother). Because evolution favors those individuals with the greatest reproductive success (the most offspring and descendants), producing sexy sons would be advantageous for a female. Good genes might also produce healthier, more vigorous offspring that are more resistant to disease and parasites. Such offspring might also be able to produce more grandchildren. Although it is not clear that genetic quality can be inherited, there is evidence from several species that females choose to

engage in extra-pair copulations with males of better quality than their mates. For example, female Black-capped Chickadees appear to seek out more dominant males for extra-pair copulations, and female House Sparrows appear to seek out males with larger, darker bibs (the dark plumage on the chin and breast) for extra-pair copulations. There is currently no evidence that female cardinals that engage in extra-pair copulations are seeking out better-quality males (for example, males with more colorful plumage or males that sing at higher rates or with greater complexity), but examination of this possibility should prove interesting.

Although some male and female cardinals pursue mixed mating strategies, the percentage of extra-pair young among cardinals is lower than that reported for many other songbirds. For example, more than half of all Purple Martin broods contain at least one extra-pair offspring. For cardinals, it may not always pay to pursue extra-pair copulations. There are at least three factors that might contribute to the relatively low rate of extra-pair paternity in cardinals. First, any increase in reproductive success that a male might achieve by pursuing extra-pair copulations must be weighed against possible increases that might result from other activities.

For example, a male pursuing extra-pair copulations has less time to feed nestlings or fledglings, and reduced feeding rates may reduce the chances that the young will survive. Many male cardinals may determine that, at least when they have nestlings or fledglings, the best strategy is to focus on parental efforts rather than extra-pair copulations.

The relatively low rates of extra-pair behavior in cardinals may also result from females' reluctance to engage in such behavior (and, as already noted, their cooperation is probably required for successful copulations). Females may not cooperate because they may achieve better reproductive success by not participating in extra-pair copulations. This may be the case if males are somehow able to determine that their mates have engaged in extra-pair copulations and, as a result, withhold parental care. Less parental care by males may mean reduced reproductive success for females because fewer of the female's offspring are likely to survive, and a female that works harder to compensate for a male's reduction in care may suffer physically and, therefore, be unable to initiate additional breeding attempts, either in the same or a future breeding season. Studies of some species, including Bobolinks and Indigo Buntings, suggest that males do not withhold parental care in response to their mates' infidelity. However, studies of other species, including Barn Swallows, suggest that males may reduce parental efforts when their mates have had opportunities to engage in extra-pair copulations. It is not known if the parental efforts of male cardinals are correlated with the likelihood that their mates have participated in extra-pair copulations.

Another reason for not engaging in extra-pair copulations is that most female cardinals have had ample opportunity to evaluate their mates and know that they are good-quality males. In resident species such as cardinals, females may have several weeks, months, or even years to evaluate males in the population, because individuals remain in an area for extended periods. With a good-quality mate, a female may be less likely to engage in copulations with other, perhaps lower-quality, males.

A third reason why cardinals may exhibit relatively low rates of extra-pair behavior is that most males engage in mate guarding behavior. Mate guarding is the close following of the female by her mate during her fertile period, and the apparent objective of such guarding is to prevent the female from engaging in extra-pair copulations. During a pair's first nesting attempt, male cardinals remain in contact with (within fifty feet of) their fertile mates an average of just over 70 percent of the time. During later breeding attempts, male cardinals guard less vigorously, remaining in contact with fertile mates an average of 50 percent of the time. Male cardinals are in contact with their mates only about 40 percent of the time before the female's fertile period and less than 20 percent of the time after the fertile period.

Mate guarding by male cardinals declines during later nesting attempts, and this change in behavior is most apparent among males with fledged young. Not surprisingly, males caring for fledged young have less time to guard mates. Although female cardinals are frequently unguarded during later nesting attempts, the frequency of extra-pair copulations does not appear to increase and may in fact decrease. Some investigators have suggested that females in multibrooded species alter their reproductive strategies from the first to the second and subsequent broods. That is, males may have proved their quality by virtue of the first nest's success, and females refrain from copulating with other males during a second nesting attempt.

The function of copulation is to introduce a male's sperm into a female's reproductive tract. In male cardinals, sperm is produced in the testes. During the nonbreeding period, the testes do not produce sperm and are very small. However, as spring approaches and days become longer (or, more precisely, the ratio of daylight to dark increases), the testes begin to increase in size and may eventually become 400 to 500 times larger. This increase occurs because the longer days stimulate the pituitary gland to produce hormones that stimulate the testes. The increasingly large testes start producing the hormone testosterone, which causes male cardinals to begin establishing territories and singing. Within the enlarging testes, seminiferous tubules increase in length and diameter and eventually begin to produce sperm. The tubes through which sperm leave the testes, the ductus (or vas) deferens, also change, with the ends forming a large mass of convolutions. These masses of convoluted tubules becomes so large in male cardinals that they form an obvious projection from the surface of the body called the cloacal protuberance. The cloacal protuberance serves one or perhaps two functions. One is to store sperm, and the other may be to facilitate sperm transfer during copulation.

The reproductive tract of a female cardinal consists of a single ovary containing several hundred to a thousand or more eggs plus an oviduct. As in males, the female reproductive tract, under the influence of pituitary hormones, exhibits a tremendous increase in size as the breeding season approaches. As it increases in size, the ovary begins to produce the hormone estrogen, which eventually stimulates females to initiate pair-bonding and other reproductive behaviors. The pituitary also releases increasing amounts of a hormone called prolactin which promotes development of a brood patch (discussed in more detail later) and stimulates females to incubate eggs and brood young.

When a male cardinal approaches a female wishing to copulate, she typically, but not always, gives a precopulatory display. During this display, the female fluffs her breast feathers, quivers her wings, and points her beak and tail upward. With the tail up, the opening into the cloaca—and therefore, into the female reproductive tract—is exposed. The male then approaches the female from behind or from the side and mounts her. The male brings his cloacal opening into contact with hers in what is often described as a cloacal kiss. The male then ejaculates, releasing several hundred million sperm into the female's cloaca. During copulation, a male cardinal may use his wings to maintain his balance on top of the female. Males may also grab the back feathers of the female with the bill to help maintain balance. Copulation takes only three to ten seconds, and both males and females may give low-volume call notes when so engaged. Once deposited in the female's cloaca, sperm begin moving up the oviduct. Assuming that there is no egg in the oviduct, some sperm may reach the infundibulum, the section of the oviduct where fertilization occurs, within fifteen minutes. However, not all sperm move up the oviduct; some move into special sperm storage tubules located in the walls of the lower portion of the oviduct. Sperm may be stored in these tubules for several days or more and appear to be released continuously. Thus, females have a constant supply of sperm ready to fertilize eggs.

Copulatory behavior begins a week or more before a female cardinal lays her first egg and peaks two to five days before egg laying begins. Such timing seems inappropriate, because eggs are available for fertilization only during egg laying, not before. Once a female begins to lay, however, sperm are largely unable to make their way up the oviduct, because the way is blocked by an egg moving down the oviduct. During egg laying, female cardinals typically lay an egg every twenty-four hours. As a result, the only time that sperm are able to move up the oviduct is immediately after an egg has been laid. At this point, another egg is ovulated and enters the infundibulum. So after a female cardinal lays an egg (and assuming that the clutch is not yet complete), introduced sperm have an open pathway up the oviduct for only about an hour or less. Because male cardinals may be engaged in other activities, such as defending the territory or chasing away intruding males, and thus be unavailable to copulate with their mates during that short window of opportunity, the best strategy is probably to copulate as much as possible before egg laying and get sperm into the storage tubules. Then, some of the continuously released sperm from those tubules will be in the infundibulum at the appropriate time to fertilize the egg.

Cardinal eggs are typically oval, but they are sometimes long or short oval. The shell is smooth, and the basic color is grayish white, buffy white, or greenish white. Eggs are usually well speckled and spotted in various shades of brown. The markings may be evenly distributed over the entire egg but are often more concentrated toward the large end. Some cardinal eggs are so thickly speckled and spotted that the basic color is almost obscured; others are only sparsely spotted. Cardinal eggs are typically twenty-five by eighteen millimeters (about one by three-quarters of an inch). Rarely, female cardinals lay eggs that are noticeably smaller than normal. These small eggs are called runt eggs and are rarely, if ever, fertile. Runt eggs have also been reported in several other species of birds, and the physiological factors involved in the production of such eggs are not clearly understood. Runt eggs are almost always found in clutches that also contain normal eggs.

Female cardinals usually begin laying eggs two or three days after completing the nest, but this interval may be anywhere from one to eight days. Females lay one egg per day, usually within an hour or two after sunrise. The eggs in a clutch are usually laid on successive days, but particularly early in the breeding season, females occasionally skip a day so that eggs are laid every other day. Complete clutches usually consist of three or four eggs but may range anywhere from one to six eggs. Clutches are generally smaller later in the breeding season, with two or three eggs being typical. In some species, and perhaps in cardinals as well, female age has an effect on clutch size, with young females laying fewer eggs than older females. Although it is not always clear why older females produce larger clutches, one possibility is that older, more experienced females are better foragers and, therefore, are in better physical condition. Because egg production is energetically expensive, females in better condition are able to lay more eggs.

Clutches may be smaller later in the breeding season because these "late" young are less likely to survive. They have less time to learn the skills, such as foraging, that allow them to survive the winter. Also, in some species (although not yet clearly demonstrated for cardinals), young produced early in the breeding season are dominant to those produced later. Being subordinates, late young might have reduced access to resources, such as food, during their first winter and, therefore, be less likely to survive. With reduced chances of survival, late young are less valuable to adults, which put less effort into producing such young. Also contributing to the smaller clutches produced later in the season may be adults' need to begin directing less effort into reproduction and more effort into preparing themselves for the upcoming winter. Adult cardinals that overextend themselves in their last breeding attempt may be in poorer physical condition as winter approaches and, as a result, less likely to survive.

As already noted, the hormones prolactin and estrogen are produced in female cardinals as egg laying approaches. Depending on the species, one or both of these hormones stimulate development of the incubation or brood patch. This patch is a bare, flaccid area of skin that covers much of the abdomen and part of the breast of female cardinals. Feathers are lost in this area, and the area swells and softens. The patch is also highly vascular, with much blood flowing into the patch when a female is incubating eggs or brooding young. The loss of feathers plus the softening and swelling permits better contact between the skin and the eggs (or, after hatching, the young), and the blood delivers heat. Male cardinals do not develop incubation patches.

Incubation, which is the application of heat to eggs, begins after female cardinals lay the last egg of a clutch. Delaying incubation until the clutch is complete helps ensure that all the eggs will hatch at about the same time. When incubating, female cardinals try to keep the eggs at a temperature of about 98 to 100 degrees Fahrenheit. Exposure to temperatures above about 106 degrees may kill developing embryos, and temperatures below about 78 degrees may stop development. Exposure to temperatures between 78 and 94 degrees can disrupt normal development. While incubating, female cardinals periodically rotate and rearrange the eggs in the nest. This movement provides equal heating thoughout each egg and prevents the shell membranes from adhering to the shell, which could interfere with hatching.

During the day, female cardinals typically incubate for about thirty-five to forty minutes at a time interspersed with breaks of five to fifteen minutes. While incubating, females hold their wings close to the body and the tail slightly elevated. Incubating females spend much time scanning the area around the nest. Periodically, females look over the edge of the nest at the ground or tilt their heads up to scan the sky. Such scanning behavior permits females to detect the approach of potential predators. After extended periods at the nest, females, perhaps to relieve discomfort associated with remaining in the same position for a long time, sometimes stand briefly, fluff their feathers, then settle back down on the eggs. Incubating females also occasionally engage in other activities, including preening, sleeping, singing, and turning the eggs. During breaks away from the nest, female cardinals defecate and spend some time foraging. This incubation schedule is flexible, with females spending more time incubating during periods of cool weather or precipitation and less time incubating during periods of warm weather. During hot weather or when direct sunlight is striking the nest, females may cease incubating but remain at the nest to shade the eggs.

Incubation is performed entirely by female cardinals. Males occasionally make brief visits to the nest and, rarely, may appear to sit on eggs, but because males have no incubation patch, no true incubation occurs.

Although males do not incubate, they provide food for the incubating female. Females are usually fed by males when away from the nest, with one study indicating that they were fed two to three times per hour. Less frequently, averaging about once every two hours, male cardinals bring food to females at the nest. The food provided by males permits females to spend more time incubating and less time foraging. When approaching an incubating female with food, the male sometimes sings, and in response, the female may leave the nest and join the male. At other times, the pair appears to use song to let the male know whether he should come to the nest. A male is more likely to come to the nest with food if the female sings before he does, and a male is more likely to stay away if he sings first and his mate responds with the same song type. Such communication allows the more colorful and conspicuous male to restrict the number of times he visits the nest, likely reducing the chances that a predator will locate the nest. A study conducted in Indiana in which males were temporarily removed from their territories lends support to this conclusion. That is, nests with eggs were more likely to avoid predation if the male was not present. Of course, a female singing from the nest could also attract predators, but because most birds do not sing from their nests, nest predators may be less likely to search for nests by listening for song than by watching the movements of parents.

When a potential predator approaches a nest with eggs, male and female cardinals are rather weak defenders. Females usually leave the nest when the predator approaches within five to ten feet. Females typically move away from the nest at a ninety-degree angle from the predator's approach and give a series of chip calls. Such behavior may focus the predator's attention away from the nest and toward the departing female. Male cardinals generally do not respond to potential predators during the incubation period. Unlike some other species, such as Eastern Bluebirds, adult cardinals do not approach the potential predator or dive at it. Rather than risk injury or death in defense of their eggs, the strategy of cardinals is apparently to renest as quickly as possible following predation.

The incubation period for cardinals is normally twelve or thirteen days. Embryos grow slowly for the first two or three days of incubation but then enter a period of rapid weight gain. The embryo's main systems—circulatory, digestive, respiratory, and nervous—begin to differentiate by the second or third day. Limb movements begin as early as the fourth day, and the egg tooth becomes apparent by the fifth or sixth day. The yolk sac gets smaller as the embryo grows. As the incubation period comes to an end, the embryonic cardinal prepares for hatching. Prior to hatching, embryos assume the tucking position, with the head oriented so that the bill lies between the body and the right wing. Then, perhaps a day or so before hatching, the young cardinal uses its bill to puncture the innermost shell membrane at the blunt end of the egg, a process referred to as internal pipping. At this location in the egg, there is a pocket of air between the inner membrane and the outer shell membrane that the young cardinal begins to breathe. After a few more hours, the young bird begins to break through the outer shell membrane and the shell, a process called external pipping. The egg tooth, near the tip of the bill, helps the young cardinal break through the shell. With external pipping, the young bird can begin breathing fresh air from the outside. Over the next several hours, the young cardinal pecks the shell while slowly rotating, producing a small circle of cracks and holes. The chick penetrates the shell at this circle and begins to emerge from the egg. The entire process, from external pipping through hatching, usually takes about twelve to sixteen hours.

Occasionally, female cardinals assist their young by removing part of the shell. Most of the time, however, adults do not assist the young in the hatching process. After hatching, the young cardinal's egg tooth is gradually absorbed and disappears. Because the female cardinal does not begin incubating until after the last egg is laid, all eggs in a clutch normally hatch within twenty-four hours, but the interval between hatching of the first and last egg may be as long as forty-eight hours. Adults either eat the eggshells or carry the shell fragments some distance from the nest and dispose of them. Removing the light-colored shell fragments from the nest makes it less likely that a predator will locate the nest.

8

Nestlings and Their Parents

At hatching, young cardinals are naked, blind, immobile, and completely dependent on their parents. All young songbirds hatch in a similar condition and are referred to as altricial young. In contrast, precocial young, like those of ducks, grouse, pheasants, and several other groups of birds, are covered with down, have open eyes, and are mobile enough to leave the nest soon after hatching. Altricial young are also unable to maintain their body temperatures. As a result, female cardinals must brood newly hatched nestlings. Thus, during the first three or four days after hatching, females are at the nest as much as they were during incubation. Male cardinals do not develop incubation or brood patches and therefore do not brood nestlings. When a female is brooding, her brood patch is

placed against the nestlings, permitting the transfer of heat to the nestlings. Nestling cardinals do not begin producing their own heat until they are about four or five days old, and their ability to maintain a constant body temperature continues to improve until they fledge. At fledging, young cardinals can maintain body temperatures nearly as well, if not as well, as adults. Because nestlings are able to generate heat and maintain their body temperatures reasonably well by about six days after hatching, female cardinals brood nestlings much less frequently after that time. Throughout the nestling period, females brood nestlings at night.

The time that a female cardinal must spend brooding young varies with temperature and brood size. Young must be brooded for longer periods when temperatures are lower, but larger broods require less brooding than smaller broods. This is true because young huddled together in a nest have less skin surface exposed and lose heat at a slower rate, and more nestlings means less exposed skin surface. So, for example, at a given environmental temperature, a brood of four nestling cardinals would need less brooding than a brood of two or a single nestling.

In addition to brooding, female cardinals may also have to shade nestlings when direct sunlight is falling on the nest. When shading young, females may simply stand in or on the nest and are not in direct contact with the young (and therefore are not transferring any heat to them).

Another behavior exhibited by female cardinals during the nestling period is referred to as "tremble-thrusting." This behavior involves thrusting the bill deep into the cup of the nest with a trembling motion. As described by one investigator, such thrusts are very forceful "and often shook the nest and the surrounding vegetation. At times the bill appeared almost to be thrust through the nest wall." Tremble-thrusts may be performed as often as three to four times per hour, particularly during the first half of the nestling period. Although its functions are not known with certainty, tremble-thrusting may help remove parasites from the nest. Females may pick up parasites in the bill when performing this behavior, and some parasites (particularly larval or pupal forms) may be shaken from the nest by the trembling movements.

Nestlings require food. Both adults feed the nestlings, but male cardinals usually provide more food than do females. When feeding nestlings, adults often forage at distances of about ten to one hundred feet from the nest but may travel farther. Investigators in Ohio monitored the nests of twenty-three pairs of cardinals throughout the nestling period and found that males made an average of 2.3 feeding trips to the nest per hour and females made an average of 1.8 trips.

It is not clear why male cardinals feed nestlings at higher rates than females, because research has demonstrated that females are able to raise nestlings in the absence of their mates. One investigator temporarily removed male cardinals from their territories when young were in the nest and found that "deserted" female cardinals compensated by increasing the rate at which they fed nestlings. As a result of this increase in female parental effort, nestlings grew at rates comparable to those in nests where both parents were feeding the young and were just as likely to survive until fledging. Interestingly, some females acquired new mates in the absence of their original mates, and these new males never helped care for the young. This is not surprising, however, because the young were not related to the new males, and birds rarely exhibit altruistic behavior. In this case, altruism would be defined as behavior that increases the reproductive success of one individual while decreasing the reproductive success or potential reproductive success of the altruist.

One possible reason why male cardinals feed nestlings at a higher rate than females is that such behavior permits females to conserve energy and prepare for another nesting attempt. Soon after a nest is lost to predators or after young successfully fledge, female cardinals typically begin construction of a new nest and, shortly thereafter, produce a new clutch of eggs. Nest building and especially egg production require a substantial input of energy by a female cardinal. A female whose mate has been the primary

provider for their nestlings may be in better physical condition and therefore better prepared to initiate a new nest and, perhaps, produce a larger clutch. If so, both the male and female would benefit, because the chances of producing more young would be improved.

A second reason why male cardinals feed nestlings at a higher rate than females is that there might be a male-biased breeding-adult sex ratio. In other words, there might be more adult males in the population than adult females. Little is known about adult sex ratios in cardinal

populations, but sex ratios are known to be male biased in other species of songbirds, Northern Mockingbirds, for example. With a male-biased sex ratio and plenty of extra males available, a female cardinal could easily change mates if her present mate provides less than the desired level of parental care. In contrast, males would have little or no opportunity to find a new mate because of the shortage of adult females. As a result, females may be able to demand more parental care from males than they would give if there were more females in the population.

In cardinals and in other species, older, larger nestlings require more food to supply sufficient energy for temperature maintenance and for additional growth. Studies of several other songbirds revealed that both adults often increase feeding rates to meet the increasing demands of older nestlings. The Ohio study, however, revealed that although male cardinals increased feeding rates as their nestlings grew older, female feeding rates remained constant. As with overall feeding rates, males may increase feeding rates to older nestlings to allow their mates to prepare for the next nesting attempt or to reduce the likelihood that their mates will seek better-quality males.

As brood size increases, male and female cardinals tend to increase feeding rates. However, the increase in feeding rates is not proportional to the increase in the number of young to be fed; as a result, individual nestlings in large broods receive less food than those in smaller broods. Similar results have been reported in several other species, including Eastern Bluebirds, Nashville Warblers, and Northern Mockingbirds. Despite being fed at somewhat lower rates, nestlings in larger broods typically grow at the same rates as those in smaller broods. This suggests that nestlings in larger broods require less food than do nestlings in smaller broods. It may be that thermoregulatory costs (the energy needed to maintain normal body temperature) are lower for nestlings in larger broods. Nestlings huddled together in a nest can share body heat, and each nestling has less exposed body surface. As brood size increases, say from three to four, the amount of exposed surface area relative to the weight of each nestling decreases.

Less exposed surface area means that less heat is lost by each nestling and, therefore, less energy—and thus less food—is needed to generate heat.

The Ohio study also revealed that the feeding rates of paired males and females were correlated. In other words, male cardinals that fed nestlings at higher rates than other males tended to be paired with females that also fed nestlings at higher rates. Such results support the "matched quality hypothesis," which predicts that mates will match in terms of the effort expended in raising young. Males and females are not necessarily predicted to match each other in terms of effort expended (for example, make the same number of feeding trips to the nest) but rather to match each other's relative effort. In other words, a female that pairs with a male whose parental efforts are average for a male in the population would be expected to match that by expending effort at the level of the average female in the population. This matching of male and female effort could occur if higher-quality individuals select only higher-quality mates or if one sex chooses mates based on some cue (such as plumage quality) that accurately predicts the level of that individual's parental effort and then simply matches that effort. Further study is needed to determine which, if either, of these factors best explains the apparently matched nestling feeding behavior of male and female cardinals.

Whereas adult cardinals feed on a variety of items, including fruits and seeds, the diet of nestlings is largely, if not entirely, insects. Almost all nestling birds are fed insects, especially during the first few days after hatching. During this early nestling period, young birds are growing rapidly. The production of new cells and tissues requires lots of protein, and insects

are richer in protein than seeds, fruits, or other plant material. Soft-bodied larvae such as caterpillars are easier to digest than hard-bodied prey such as cicadas, beetles, or grasshoppers and may contain the nutrients needed by very young birds. The digestive systems of young birds may become more efficient with increasing age, permitting adults to provide older nestlings with more hard-bodied insect prey. To further help very young nestlings digest their food, adult cardinals crush insect prey in their bills before giving it to their young. Only late in the nestling period or after fledging do adult cardinals begin to feed their young any plant material.

As is the case with all songbird nestlings, young cardinals solicit food from their parents by begging. When begging, nestling cardinals utter vocalizations, referred to as begging calls, and simultaneously extend their heads upward with their mouths wide open. In very young nestlings, any movement of the nest is enough to stimulate begging. However, as they grow older, nestlings learn to ignore incidental movements and usually respond only to the vocalizations or presence of their parents. Although there have been no detailed studies of the begging behavior of young cardinals, studies of other songbird nestlings indicate that the nestling that starts to beg first, reaches highest, and holds its beak closest to the parent is most likely to be fed. Previous studies provided little evidence that adults selectively feed particular nestlings. In other words, adults do not keep track of which nestlings they feed or make sure that all young receive similar amounts of food. Adult songbirds simply feed the nestling that begs most vigorously. Typically, begging intensity is related to a nestling's hunger level, with begging intensity increasing as the time since the last feeding increases. Thus, nestlings fed most recently tend to beg less vigorously, as a result, all nestlings usually receive similar amounts of food from their parents.

Surprisingly, begging calls appear to have little to do with determining which nestling will be fed. Rather, it is the nestling's position (and, more precisely, the position of the nestling's open mouth) that determines whether it will be fed. If so, why utter begging calls that could attract a predator to the nest? One interesting study with Great Tits (a European species related to North American chickadees and titmice) revealed that adults increased their feeding rates when prerecorded begging calls were played back over speakers near the nests.

Other studies revealed that calling rates of nestlings are correlated with their hunger level. So it appears that adult songbirds use the collective vocalizing of their nestlings to assess the nestlings' hunger level, permitting adults to adjust feeding rates to the hunger level of their broods. Adults bring enough food to ensure that their young continue to grow as they should, but they do not bring more food than is necessary. Bringing too much food would waste parental energy, and more parental visits to the nest could increase the chances of a predator noticing the activity and locating the nest.

Nestling cardinals produce lots of fecal material, and this material must be removed from the nest by the parents. Such nest sanitation is important for a variety of reasons. The nest must be kept dry and warm to maintain its insulating capacity. Also, an accumulation of fecal material in the nest would provide a perfect environment for bacteria and parasites that could infest the nestlings and cause illness or even death. Accumulating fecal material in or around the nest could also attract potential nest predators, either because of the odor or, especially for avian predators, because of the obvious white color of the feces. Nest sanitation is made easier for adult songbirds, including cardinals, because the fecal material of nestlings is enclosed in a tough mucous membrane and forms what is called a fecal sac.

During the first four or five days of the nestling period, adult cardinals eat most of the fecal sacs produced by their nestlings. Such behavior not only helps keep the nest clean but also provides the adults with some nutritional benefit. Food passing through the digestive systems of young birds is not completely digested, so the feces have some nutritional value. For example, one study revealed that fecal sacs eaten by adult White-crowned Sparrows provided as much as 10 percent of their daily energy needs. Fecal sacs produced by older nestlings apparently have little nutritional value and are not consumed by adults. Typically, adults carry these fecal sacs some distance from the nest and then drop them.

Each nestling usually produces a fecal sac after being fed three or four times, and sacs are usually expelled right after being fed. Adults, especially females, often remain at the nest after feeding a nestling and wait for the fecal sac to be expelled. Often, the nestling leans forward while an adult—again, usually a female—gently pokes the nestling near the cloaca to stimulate ejection of a fecal sac.

The wings of nestling cardinals develop more slowly than do the mouth or legs. Young cardinals are not capable of even limited flight, flying short distances downward, until about eleven or twelve days old. Thereafter, their ability to fly gradually improves, and they may be capable of short horizontal flights at about fourteen or fifteen days old. Thus, whereas young cardinals need longer, stronger legs as soon as possible to permit more efficient begging, rapid development of the wings is not as important.

As nestlings develop, the eyes gradually open (three to five days after hatching), and their juvenal plumage begins to develop. Although they will eventually cover the entire body, feathers are not distributed uniformly. Rather, feathers originate from regions of skin called feather tracts (pterylae), which are separated from other such regions by areas of skin with few or no feathers (apteria). Two to four days after hatching, feather sheaths emerge from the various feather tracts, including those on the wings and tail. As these new feathers emerge, the natal down is pushed out and is gradually lost. Four or five days after hatching, the primary wing feathers break through the distal portions of their sheaths, and about a day later, feathers emerge from sheaths in other feather tracts. Thereafter, the body feathers grow rapidly and largely cover the apteria by ten days after

hatching. By that time, the primaries are about two-thirds the length of adult primaries and will continue to grow after fledging. The tail feathers (rectrices) emerge after the wing feathers and grow more slowly. As the nestling period draws to a close ten to eleven days after hatching, the tail feathers of nestling cardinals are only about one-quarter the length of adult tail feathers.

During the first three or four days after hatching, nestling cardinals are brooded much of the time, and they do very little beyond raising their heads and gaping when an adult arrives at the nest with food. Although levels of activity increase somewhat with increasing age, nestlings at all stages spend most of their time simply resting and growing. Very young cardinals vocalize, producing low-volume, high-frequency begging calls. With increasing age, these calls become louder and lower in frequency. Nestlings are able to use their wings to help hold themselves up when they are about three days old. By four to five days after hatching, nestling cardinals exhibit improving muscular coordination and are able to stand and orient toward parents when they arrive at the nest. Nestlings may also begin preening their developing feathers. By six or seven days after hatching, young cardinals can grasp objects firmly with their feet and also begin to exercise their wings. By the eighth or ninth day after hatching, nestlings are becoming more alert to events outside the nest and may even leave the nest if disturbed. The volume of begging calls is now at its loudest. At this stage, young cardinals are also able to perch, although some-what unsteadily. Nestlings are doing more stretching and exercising of their legs and wings and spend more time preening. Young cardinals usually leave the nest, or fledge, about ten or eleven days after hatching.

During the nestling period, siblings compete indirectly, with each nestling doing its best to obtain food from parents visiting the nest. However, there is no direct aggression among siblings—no direct sibling rivalry. Direct aggression among siblings does occur in some species and may cause the death of one or more nestlings. This behavior is referred to as siblicide. The young of nonsiblicidal species such as cardinals—do not have the "weapons"—hooked or long, pointed bills—needed to kill nest mates.

Cowbirds are well-known brood parasites—species in which females lay their eggs in the nests of other species. Two species are known to parasitize cardinals: the Bronzed Cowbird, with a range that includes the southwestern United States, Mexico, and Central America, and the Brown-headed Cowbird, which ranges throughout much of North America. Brown-headed Cowbirds have been reported to parasitize over 200 species of birds, including Northern Cardinals. Most female cowbirds lay thirty to forty eggs each breeding season and usually lay two to five eggs per week. Although individual female cowbirds deposit only one egg per nest, more than one female may lay an egg in the same nest. As a result, host nests sometimes contain two or more cowbird eggs and, later, two or more cowbird nestlings. Cowbirds nestlings typically hatch before the host nestlings and, because of this head start, are usually larger than the host nestlings. Being larger, cowbird nestlings obtain more of the food being delivered by parents.

One study in Ohio revealed that 48 percent of Northern Cardinal nests were parasitized by Brown-headed Cowbirds, and these parasitized nests generally contained one or two cowbird eggs or young. Parasitized cardinal nests sometimes had fewer eggs than nonparasitized nests because female cowbirds occasionally remove a host egg before laying their own egg. Despite this egg removal, there was no difference in the number of young cardinals that fledged from parasitized and nonparasitized nests. Also, unlike other species, nestling cardinals in parasitized weighed as much as nestlings in nonparasitized nests. These results suggest that, at least in some areas, cowbird parasitism has little or no impact on cardinal nestling success.

Young cardinals typically fledge about ten or eleven days after hatching. Among songbirds, the duration of the nestling period is influenced by size—with larger species having longer nestling periods—and by nest location. Species, such as cardinals, that are open nesters (that is, build an open-cup nest) have shorter nestling periods than cavity nesters. Whereas an eleven-day nestling period is typical for an open-nesting species, nestling periods for cavity nesters of comparable size are about nineteen days. This difference appears to be influenced at least in part by the risk of nest failure. Open-cup nesters may suffer higher rates of nest predation; as a result, it is beneficial for young to leave the nest as soon as possible. In a related vein,

cardinals and many other open nesters are multibrooded, perhaps in part to compensate for high rates of nest predation. Shorter nesting cycles, including shorter nestling periods improve the chances of producing, or at least attempting to produce, multiple broods.

What actually induces young cardinals to leave the nest? One important factor is size. Nestlings must achieve a particular level of maturation or development before they can survive outside of the nest. For example, a nestling that leaves the nest before it is able to maintain its body temperature or before it has sufficient muscular control to maintain its position on a perch almost certainly will not survive. Once that level of development has been reached, the primary factors involved in determining the time of fledging are probably energy considerations (hunger) and sibling competition. In other words, nestlings probably leave the nest in an attempt to approach parents and obtain additional feedings at the expense of siblings. Once one nestling has left the nest, parents may preferentially feed that nestling. Siblings remaining in the nest are not fed or at least are not fed as frequently. Energy considerations then stimulate them to follow their newly fledged sibling and leave the nest themselves.

9

Fledging and the Postfledging Period

As the time of nest departure approaches, young cardinals first perch on the rim of the nest or on a branch immediately adjacent to the nest. They may remain in this position for an hour or more but eventually move farther from the nest. Nestlings often leave the nest, or fledge, late in the morning but may do so at any time of the day. All young in a nest may leave within an hour or less, but departure of the entire brood may take up to twenty-four hours.

At fledging, young cardinals are not capable of extended flights because their flight feathers and flight muscles are not completely developed. Initial flights may be as short as four or five feet or as long as thirty to forty feet, but they average about fifteen feet in length. During these early flights, young cardinals have difficulty maintaining lift and, as a result, almost always lose altitude and end up on the ground or in the lower part of a bush or tree. If initial flights end on the ground, young cardinals hop or make short flights into nearby shrubs or trees.

During the first ten days after fledging, young cardinals change locations infrequently. Most of the time, they remain on perches about five to fifteen feet high in a shrub or tree, within ten to thirty feet of the nest and, often, of one another. Commonly, perches chosen by newly fledged cardinals are not well concealed. However, because the juvenal plumage of fledglings is largely brown, and their bills are largely black rather than the reddish orange of adults, young cardinals are difficult to see when perched in a shrub or tree. Making it even more difficult to locate them is the fact that recently fledged young are also relatively immobile. These characteristics make it less likely that predators will be able to spot fledglings.

Only when adults approach do fledglings attempt to make their location known. Upon spotting or hearing a nearby adult, fledglings immediately start calling. To alert young to their presence, approaching adults typically utter one or more chip calls. The calls given by fledglings are similar to those given during the last few days of the nestling period but are often given at a faster rate and with greater volume. Unlike nestlings, fledglings can and do move about, and these characteristics of their begging calls make

the fledglings easy to locate. In addition to vocalizing, fledglings initiate a begging display during which the head is drawn back between the wings, the legs are flexed, and the body is lowered. At the same time, fledglings gape, fluff their feathers, and lift and extend their wings while moving them rapidly up and down (wing quivering). As an adult gets closer, the intensity of the fledgling's begging display increases and reaches a peak just prior to being fed. As the adult departs, the fledgling continues to beg, but the intensity of the display gradually diminishes. After being fed several times, and as hunger levels decline, fledglings call and display with reduced vigor and may simply wing quiver without uttering any calls. Between feedings, fledglings are usually quiet, but if they are still hungry, fledglings may continue to utter begging calls, although at a lower rate and volume than when adults are nearby.

Recently fledged young respond to an approaching predator (including an approaching human) by crouching and, if calling, by becoming quiet. During the first ten days or so after leaving the nest, young cardinals are incapable of prolonged flight. During this time, fledglings hesitate to fly, and potential predators can approach rather closely, generally within a few feet. Once they are within that distance, however, fledglings usually fly from their perches and call loudly. These flights are short, generally no more than ten to fifteen feet, and fledglings

usually end up either on the ground or low in a shrub or tree. Fledglings do not always fly, and predators, including humans, can sometimes capture them. If captured, young cardinals immediately begin uttering loud distress calls. Adults usually respond quickly to the calls of fledglings and approach the predator. As is typical of cardinals, however, adults remain a relatively safe distance from the predator (at least five feet away, and usually more) and utter chip calls. The presence of the adults may distract the predator, but more likely, the fledgling or fledglings will be lost to the predator, unless, of course, that predator is simply a curious human. One advantage of fledging as soon as possible is that a predator is much less likely to capture all the young because fledglings, unlike nestlings, are not all in the same spot.

Gradually, fledglings become stronger and, as their flight feathers and flight muscles continue to develop, better fliers. By about ten to twelve days after fledging, young cardinals can fly reasonably well and begin to perch higher in shrubs and trees. They also begin to follow their parents in an attempt to increase the chances of being fed. In contrast to their behavior shortly after fledging, fledglings at this stage are more vocal and much more mobile. Particularly when parents approach territory boundaries, fledglings are likely to trespass onto the territories of neighboring cardinals. Neighboring adults usually show little aggression toward trespassing fledglings but respond with aggression if the parents also trespass while trying to feed their young.

Young cardinals make their first attempts at foraging for themselves about ten to twelve days after fledging. Early attempts to capture prey are usually unsuccessful, but with increasing age and practice, success rates gradually improve. Because of their mobility, fledgling cardinals at this stage are difficult to observe. Thus, little is known about the process whereby young cardinals develop their foraging skills. Certain aspects of foraging are probably innate. For example, the movements involved in using the bill to capture prey probably require little learning. In contrast, when it comes to learning where to forage and what items to select as prey, some learning is likely involved. Some of this learning is probably trial and error, but fledglings may also acquire important information by following their parents and noting where they forage and what types of food they select.

Another important skill that young cardinals must acquire is the ability to recognize and avoid predators. Little is known about the acquisition of this ability in cardinals, but studies of other species revealed that predator recognition may be partly innate. For example, there is evidence that young birds have an innate ability to recognize aerial predators such as hawks and perhaps owls. It is also likely, however, that young cardinals learn to identify and respond to certain predators by observing the responses of their parents. For example, adult cardinals may utter chip notes and other vocalizations or seek cover at the approach of a potential predator and, in so doing, provide their young with valuable information. Cardinals, along with several other species of birds, also occasionally engage in mobbing behavior. When a potential predator, such as an owl or a snake, is discovered, cardinals, often joined by chickadees or titmice, remain nearby and utter loud chip calls. Mobbing behavior may serve a variety of functions, including alerting mates or young to the presence of the predator. Young cardinals that participate may also be learning to recognize the mobbed predators.

By about twenty to twenty-five days after fledging, young cardinals are becoming increasingly independent. Fledglings at this age still spend time following and being fed by their parents, but they also begin to move throughout the territory, and into adjacent territories on their own. At this stage, their foraging skills are continuing to improve, but many if not most attempts at capturing insects or other prey are still unsuccessful. Because of their limited foraging success, hungry fledglings are likely to solicit food from their parents. Then, after being fed, they may continue with their own less efficient attempts to find food. Fledglings are now fed, or may obtain themselves, a greater variety of food items. Insects are still the predominant food, supplemented with berries and seeds. Fledglings forage both in shrubs and trees and on the ground. Occasionally, young cardinals attempt to capture prey located on small limbs or leaves while hovering. When reaching for small insects from a perch, inexperienced cardinals sometimes overextend themselves and lose their balance. Learning to forage efficiently may take several months, and even after becoming independent, young cardinals are not able to forage as well as adults. Such inefficiency no doubt contributes to the high mortality rates experienced by young birds, including cardinals, during their first year of life.

Young cardinals usually become independent of their parents about forty days after leaving the nest. Young that fledge early in the breeding season generally become independent at an earlier age than do those that fledge from the last nest of the season. This is so because the

young from early nests may be driven from the territory by parents that have renested and have new broods of nestlings to feed. In contrast, late in the season, adults do not renest and may care for fledglings longer. Late in a breeding season, one investigator observed adult cardinals still feeding young fifty-six days after fledging.

When attempting to drive their young from the territory, adults fly at them and displace them from perches while giving loud chip calls. Despite this parental aggression, fledglings may persist in begging from parents. Parents, however, persist in their attempts to evict the young and continue to display aggression whenever fledglings approach them or the new nest. Generally, after two or three days of such treatment, the fledglings leave the parental territory and initiate dispersal. Young that fledge from the last nest of the season are not driven from parental territories. Rather, about forty to fifty days after fledging, adults simply begin to ignore all attempts by their young to solicit food. These young may remain in or near parental territories into September or even October and may join their parents as flocks begin to form. However, all young cardinals eventually initiate dispersal.

After fledging of their young, adult cardinals sometimes divide the brood. In some species that exhibit brood division, one adult takes some fledglings to one part of the territory, and the other adult takes the rest to another part of the territory. In cardinals and other species, however, the division is less definite. All fledglings may remain in the same general area, and one adult primarily feeds certain young while the other adult primarily feeds the others. In addition, adults sometimes "trade" fledglings. If there is only a single fledgling, both parents help care for it.

Early in the breeding season (May through July), females aid their mates in caring for young for about eighteen to twenty days after fledging. At this stage, young cardinals are beginning to spend time away from their parents and, to a limited degree, forage for themselves. With this decreased dependence, the adult male can care for the fledglings alone, and the female can start building the next nest. If there is only one fledgling to care for, males can assume responsibility more quickly, and females may begin the next nest just thirteen or fourteen days after fledging.

Although adults typically feed each recently fledged young about eight times per hour, feeding rates can range from just once or twice per hour to fifteen or more times per hour. Adults continue to feed young at these rates for about ten to twelve days after fledging. At that point, feeding rates begin to slowly decline as young become able to obtain some food on their own. In addition to feeding young, adults do their best to protect them from potential predators. Recently fledged young frequently utter begging calls to solicit food from parents, and this calling can attract predators. One important means of protecting fledglings is to discourage them from calling when a predator is nearby. Adults do this by uttering loud chip calls. Upon hearing these calls, fledged young become silent almost immediately.

For the first week to ten days after fledging, young cardinals generally move very little. Parents occasionally attempt to lead their fledglings to new locations in the territory, perhaps to find better cover, to be closer to foraging areas, or to move away from potential predators. To encourage following, the adult glides away from fledglings in the appropriate direction with spread wings and tail. If the fledglings fail to respond, the adult returns and repeats the display. Once the flying skills of fledglings have improved, adults may encourage them to follow by simply flying in the desired direction and, upon reaching a perch, giving chip calls.

All young cardinals eventually leave parental territories, either as a result of parental aggression or on their own, and move to another location where they eventually breed—if they survive. This movement of young birds is called natal dispersal. Very little is known about the natal dispersal of cardinals, but in general, young songbirds disperse relatively short distances, and the vast majority of young cardinals probably move less than a mile from parental territories. Studies of young cardinals that have been banded to permit the identification of individual birds, using numbered aluminum tags that fit like a bracelet on one leg, revealed that a few juveniles may move much farther—in extreme cases, one hundred miles or more. Natal dispersal poses potential risks. For example, young birds moving through

unfamiliar areas are particularly vulnerable to predation. However, natal dispersal also provides benefits. Moving away from parents and siblings decreases the chances of breeding with near relatives and thus decreases the chances of inbreeding. In addition, young cardinals may disperse into areas with improved opportunities for obtaining needed resources, such as a breeding territory or a mate.

In many species of birds, including cardinals, young females tend to disperse farther than young males. The reasons for such sex-biased dispersal are not completely understood, but the mating system of cardinals and many other songbirds may be one important factor. Male cardinals establish breeding territories that contain resources essential to successful reproduction, and females choose mates based, at least in part, on differences in the quality of these territories. Young males remaining near their natal territories may be more likely to establish a good-quality territory because familiarity with the area permits higher feeding rates and lower predation rates. In other words, males remaining as close as possible to their natal territories are more likely to survive and are more likely to be in good physical condition. Young females, in contrast, might benefit from "sampling" a greater number of potential mates and, particularly if inbreeding is detrimental, travel greater distances as they seek good-quality mates and territories.

During dispersal, young cardinals may temporarily join flocks consisting of other juveniles plus a few adults. Dispersing young may remain in a particular area or flock for just a few hours or days. If, however, a young cardinal finds an area with abundant food and shelter, further dispersal may be delayed for many days or even weeks. Before completing dispersal, it is likely that young male cardinals evaluate areas as potential territories; young females, particularly as spring approaches, remain on the lookout for potential mates.

After fledging, the main flight feathers (primaries and secondaries) and the tail feathers (rectrices) of young cardinals continue to grow. Within a week to ten days, the flight feathers have completed their growth. The tail feathers grow more slowly and may not be completely developed until about three weeks after fledging. While these flight and tail feathers are growing, young male and female cardinals begin a molt the presupplemental molt, a molt of most or all of the remaining body feathers that lasts for three to four weeks. During this molt, the female-like juvenal plumage is replaced with another female-like plumage referred to as the supplemental plumage.

The fate of the supplemental plumage is largely determined by a young cardinal's hatching date. Young that hatch early in the breeding season (May and June) generally retain the supplemental plumage until sometime in July or August. At that point, the first prebasic molt begins. A complete first prebasic molt takes anywhere from about twelve to seventeen weeks and involves replacement of all body feathers, including primaries, secondaries, and rectrices. Some young cardinals, especially those that hatch later in the breeding season (July and August), have insufficient time to complete this first prebasic molt before the onset of winter (mid- to late November). These juveniles undergo a partial first prebasic molt, replacing most or all body feathers but not replacing all primaries, secondaries, and rectrices. By not having to replace these feathers, young cardinals conserve energy that can be used to generate more body feathers. In fact, observations have revealed that late-hatched cardinals that retain some flight feathers and rectrices develop additional down feathers in what are normally unfeathered areas (the apteria), as do young that undergo a complete molt. The additional insulation provided by these down feathers is no doubt useful in retaining body heat during cold weather.

The first prebasic molt typically ends by mid-November, and with the completion of this molt, the plumage of young cardinals resembles that of adults and is called the first basic plumage. Beginning prior to and continuing after the completion of this molt, bill color also changes. Young cardinals have black bills, but beginning a few weeks after fledging, the bills gradually change to the adultlike orange-red color. This change in bill color requires two to three months, and even for late-hatched young, it is completed by mid- to late December. Thus, by the end of December, young males and females have attained an adult appearance.

Attainment of the first basic plumage represents little change for young females, because this plumage is similar to the supplementary plumage. Both are primarily light brown tinged with a bit of red, especially on the crest, wings, and tail. These are the relatively drab plumages that help females blend into the background and reduce the likelihood that they will be seen by potential predators. In contrast, the first prebasic molt transforms young males from drab to bright red, making them more likely to be spotted by potential predators. That, of course, represents a potential disadvantage, but the bright red plumage may also enhance the competitive ability of young males during their first winter. For example, observations of cardinals at feeding stations have revealed that males are

usually dominant over females. As a result, males can displace females and gain access to food. Young males' bright red plumage thus improves their access to important resources.

First-year birds, especially small songbirds, typically suffer high mortality rates, and young cardinals are no exception. It is likely that 70 to 90 percent of young cardinals die during their first year of life. During the nestling period and shortly after fledging, high mortality rates are caused primarily by predation. Nestlings and recently fledged young are incapable of flight (or at least of sustained flight). In addition, very young cardinals are not as vigilant as adults. For example, recently fledged cardinals may continue to utter begging calls even when a predator is in the vicinity. As a result, nestlings and recently fledged cardinals suffer high rates of predation. Another period of high mortality occurs immediately after parents stop feeding fledglings.

If young cardinals become sufficiently proficient at foraging to survive the first two or three weeks of independence, their chances of surviving until the next breeding season improve dramatically. Predators, such as hawks and owls, will continue to take some young cardinals throughout the winter, and some birds, particularly in harsh winters, may die of starvation, but after the first weeks of juvenile independence, mortality rates for first-year cardinals probably decline and approach those for adults. However, even for adult cardinals, mortality rates are probably about 40 percent. Thus, most cardinals live only two to five years. Rarely, cardinals live as long as ten to fifteen years.

10

The Nonbreeding Period

By late September, little or no singing is heard, and as the month progresses, defense of territory boundaries diminishes before becoming nonexistent. Also in September, flocks of cardinals begin to form. Initially, flocks may be family units, consisting of a pair plus young from their last nest. Cardinals continue to utilize the same areas but begin to range outside the former boundaries. Adult males continue to spend much of their time in their former territories, but females and especially juveniles range over a larger area and spend more time in flocks with other cardinals. Juveniles continue to range farther from their natal territories and begin dispersing. Adults can also be rather mobile during the nonbreeding period, but some pairs maintain sufficient contact to prevent complete dissolution of the pair-bond, and these pairs may be among the first to start spending more time together during late winter (January and February) in preparation for the next breeding season.

Once each year, adult cardinals undergo molt, a process by which old feathers are replaced with new ones. Such replacement is necessary because feathers are nonliving structures and, over time, gradually begin to show signs of wear and tear. These old feathers must be replaced because structurally sound feathers are needed for efficient flight and thermoregulation. In addition, plumage quality and color can be important indicators of sex, age, and condition, and old, faded feathers may not accurately signal this information.

Adult cardinals typically begin molting sometime from mid-August to early September. Because cardinals are multibrooded, adults are often caring for nestlings or fledglings when molt begins. Both caring for young and molting can take substantial amounts of energy, and minimizing the overlap between these two activities would seem to be beneficial. Particularly in their northern range, however, adults must initiate molting before their young are independent so that it will be complete by the time temperatures begin to fall. When parental care and molting overlap, the energy needs of adults are very high. Fortunately, food in the form of seeds, fruits, and insects is typically abundant at this time, permitting most adult cardinals to meet their energy requirements.

Molt is a gradual process and generally takes about four to six weeks. Thus, most adult cardinals complete molt by sometime in October. Feathers of a particular area, or feather tract, are not shed all at once, and within each feather tract, the sequence of feather loss is consistent from bird to bird. For example, molt of the tail feathers generally begins with the loss of the innermost two feathers. As these two new feathers begin to grow out, the two adjacent feathers are lost, and so on, until finally the outermost tail feathers are lost. By the time the outermost tail feathers are lost, replacement of the innermost feathers is nearing completion.

Because molt of the feathers needed for flight is gradual and symmetrical, cardinals are always able to fly. The loss of body feathers reduces the insulating capacity of the plumage, but molt is almost always finished by early November, before the coldest temperatures arrive.

Adult cardinals are generally sedentary but, particularly during the fall and winter, they sometimes exhibit breeding dispersal. Breeding dispersal is the movement of adults that have reproduced to successive breeding sites. In most species of birds, females are more likely to make these movements than males. A male may be forced to disperse if he loses his territory to another male. A female cardinal may disperse if her mate from the previous breeding season dies or is killed by a predator or if she is divorced by or chooses to divorce a previous mate. Although carrying obvious human connotations, the term "divorce" is widely used among ornithologists when referring to cases in which at least one partner re-pairs with another individual while both original partners are still alive. Cardinal pairs sometimes persist for two or more years, but others do not.

At least two factors might lead to divorce in cardinals and other species of birds. First, divorce may occur when one member of a pair has the opportunity to obtain a better-quality mate. In such cases, the divorce may not be the result of lack of prior reproductive success but rather the probability of improved reproductive success. A second possibility is that divorce is caused by the intrusion of a third individual that displaces one member of the pair. This could occur if the third individual, the new mate, is dominant over the ousted partner. If a divorce occurs late in the breeding season, the displaced individual may disperse during the nonbreeding season and, while doing so, evaluate other individuals as potential mates. During breeding dispersal, adult cardinals rarely travel long distances, with most going less than a mile.

Both dispersing and nondispersing cardinals join flocks. Cardinal flocks are temporary aggregations, particularly for adults. Cardinals spend most of their time in flocks, but the composition of those flocks changes continuously. For example, adult males and females may join a flock as it passes through or near their range but drop out as the flock moves beyond their normal range. If another flock passes nearby sometime later, adults may temporarily join that flock. Unlike the flocks of some other species of birds, cardinal flocks have no permanent membership. Unlike adults, juveniles have no former territory and range more widely during the nonbreeding season. Juveniles are also more likely to remain in flocks for extended periods.

Cardinal flocks usually consist of about five to twenty individuals, but they may be smaller or larger. In areas where cardinals are more abundant, such as the southeastern United States, flocks may be much larger. In fact, flocks of sixty or more cardinals have been observed, but flocks that large are unusual. The size of cardinal flocks varies during the winter: It generally increases through the fall, peaks in December and January, then declines into February and March. At least two factors contribute to this variation in flock size. First, beginning in late summer and continuing through the fall, male and female cardinals spend less time on their former territories and more time in flocks. Then, beginning in February, females and particularly males begin forming pairs and establishing territories and, as a result, again spend less time in flocks.

A second factor is weather. As temperatures decline, the size of cardinal flocks tends to increase. In addition, cardinals may be more likely to join flocks when there is snow on the ground. Individuals in several species are more likely to join flocks when energy constraints are most severe, such as during periods of cold weather. Flock size increases as temperatures decline because birds, including cardinals, need more energy and, therefore, more food when it is colder. Cardinals concentrate in greater numbers at good feeding areas during cold weather, and individual birds in a flock can decrease the amount of time spent looking out for potential predators because the total time spent scanning by the flock is high. Less time spent looking for predators means more time available for foraging, an important factor during cold weather. It is also likely that members of a flock can locate food by watching other flock members.

The size of cardinal flocks also varies with habitat, because of variation in the distribution of food and cover. Flocks are larger in areas with abundant food and cover. In towns and cities, large flocks may be found where there are feeding stations in association with vegetative cover. Time of day also influences flock size. Cardinal flocks are larger during the morning, smaller during the afternoon, and larger again late in the afternoon. This variation is probably correlated with cardinal feeding activity, with flocks being largest when cardinals are

actively feeding. Cardinals often begin feeding before other species early in the morning and continue feeding later in the day, after other species have already entered their evening roosts. At feeding stations, for example, cardinals are typically the first birds to arrive in the morning and the last birds to leave at the end of the day. These are important feeding times, especially during cold weather. Feeding at sunset provides energy that will be used during the night, and feeding at sunrise provides needed energy after the nightly fast.

Cardinals sometimes associate with other species of birds. At various times and locations, these interspecific flocks may include Dark-eyed Juncos, White-throated Sparrows, Tufted Titmice, Song Sparrows, Black-capped or Carolina Chickadees, Tree Sparrows, White-crowned Sparrows, Rufous-sided Towhees, American Goldfinches, and other species. These flocks provide some of the same advantages as flocks made up entirely of cardinals, such as helping individuals find food or locate and evade predators. Cardinals do not appear to seek out the company of other species; rather, when they are found together, it is likely that cardinals and individuals of other species have simply been attracted to the same location by a needed resource such as food or shelter.

Although cardinals are usually in flocks during the nonbreeding season, they are occasionally found alone. Males are found alone about 25 percent of the time and females about 15 percent of the time. These solitary cardinals are usually resting in thickets or other dense vegetation. Particularly during warmer periods and at midday, cardinals may not move from good cover sites for several hours. Similarly, during the night, cardinals typically roost in dense vegetation, either alone or within five to ten feet of a few other individuals. By spending time in dense thickets where they are not easily seen and are protected from the wind and precipitation, cardinals remain hidden from predators while conserving energy.

Conserving energy can be extremely important for cardinals, particularly during cold weather. Birds are endothermic, or warm-blooded, and when active, they maintain a body temperature of 105 to 108 degrees Fahrenheit (41 to 42 degrees Celsius). Maintaining body temperature requires energy, and the amount of energy needed changes as ambient temperature changes. Cardinals expend relatively little energy when the temperature is above 64 degrees Fahrenheit. Above this temperature, cardinals can control body temperature by changing feather position, fluffing up feathers as the temperature declines and changing patterns of blood flow, directing blood away from the body surface so that less heat is lost. When the temperature drops below 64 degrees, cardinals must generate more heat and, therefore, use more energy. Throughout much of their range, winter temperatures are lower than this—often much lower—so for much of the winter, cardinals must generate more heat and use more energy. As the temperature falls, cardinals first tense their muscles, especially their breast and leg muscles, and begin to shiver. This muscular activity creates heat, but it also uses

energy. The colder the temperature, the more energy cardinals must use to stay warm. Finding and staying in microclimates that provide slightly warmer temperatures and protection from the elements can help a cardinal conserve substantial amounts of energy. Unlike some birds, cardinals do not use cavities in trees or burrow into deep snow. Cardinals do, however, roost in dense clumps of evergreens or other vegetation. To further conserve energy at night, cardinals, as is true for many birds that occupy cold climates, allow their body temperatures to drop 3 to 6 degrees Fahrenheit. Laboratory experiments have revealed that captive cardinals start having trouble maintaining body temperature when the ambient temperature drops below about 0 degrees Fahrenheit, but it is apparent that cardinals in the wild are able to survive temperatures well below that. Access to sufficient food and cover is no doubt essential in permitting cardinals to survive extended periods of cold weather.

During the nonbreeding period, cardinals may range over a substantial area. Of course, some cardinals are dispersing and may travel many miles, but most cardinals, especially adults, are a bit more sedentary. A study in Kentucky revealed that cardinals in a rural area typically ranged over ten to fifteen acres during the winter months. In Kansas, male cardinals were found to occupy ranges about twelve acres in size, whereas females occupied ranges of about twenty acres. These ranges represented the area used over an entire winter. Over shorter periods, smaller areas were used. For example, the daily ranges of cardinals in Kentucky averaged about three acres. However, the size of these daily ranges varies considerably from individual to individual and from day to day. Some cardinals, particularly adult males, are rather sedentary, and their daily ranges may average only an acre or two. Others, particularly juveniles, are more mobile, and their daily ranges may average as much as four or five acres.

Because there is no active defense of boundaries, the winter ranges of individual cardinals, unlike breeding territories, may overlap considerably during the nonbreeding period. Although there is limited information concerning the extent to which the winter ranges of cardinals overlap, the ranges of adult males probably overlap less than do the ranges of adult females or juveniles of either sex. This is not because adult males are defending their ranges but because they are more sedentary and are thus less likely to move into the ranges of other individuals.

Although ranges overlap and are not defended, cardinals seeking access to resources are sometimes involved in aggressive interactions with other individuals. Throughout the winter, such interactions may occur when two or more individuals simultaneously try to obtain the same resource. Usually, that resource is food, but cardinals may also engage in interactions when seeking access to other resources such as water or roost sites. These resources are typically distributed throughout an area. For example, seeds may be distributed relatively evenly throughout a field. In such cases, direct interactions among cardinals are uncommon, because individuals usually know their status relative to others and, under most circumstances, will not directly challenge individuals with higher status than their own. Thus, lower-ranked cardinals usually do not attempt to drive away a higher-ranked cardinal, and lower-ranked individuals usually move away at the approach of a higher-ranked individual.

Several factors may determine an individual cardinal's status or rank relative to others. Two important factors are sex and age. Male cardinals are usually dominant to females, and older cardinals are usually dominant to first-year birds. Similar relationships have been found in many other species of birds. Within sex and age classes, the factors that influence status are not always apparent. One factor that may influence the outcome of such interactions is the location. Observations have revealed that status among male cardinals is site dependent; that is, males are more likely to win encounters with other males when they are near or in

their former breeding territories. So an adult male competing for food or other resources is more likely to win if the encounter takes place in an area that was part of his previous year's breeding territory. If the same two males encounter each other in another location, the outcome may be different. It is likely, although not yet demonstrated, that adult females exhibit similar behavior.

Another factor that might influence the outcome of interactions among cardinals is plumage quality. Studies of other species revealed that variation in certain plumage characteristics can play a role in determining an individual's status. For example, among Harris' Sparrows, individuals with the most extensive and darkest plumage on the head and breast tend to be more dominant and are usually able to displace individuals with less extensive and lighter plumage. This is referred to as status signaling, and one advantage to such a system is that individuals may be better able to determine the status of others and, by doing so, avoid interactions. No such behavior has yet been described in cardinals, but cardinal plumage does exhibit some individual variation. Obviously, males and females differ in plumage, but there is also intrasexual plumage variation. Although this variation is less obvious, careful examination reveals that some males, for example, have darker red plumage than do other males. To date, no one has demonstrated that such variation is important in status signaling, but it is likely that this plumage variation serves some function, and status signaling is one possibility.

When needed resources are clumped together, interactions between cardinals are much more frequent. This is what occurs, for example, at bird feeders. At feeders, food is often abundant and, unlike in more natural environments, is found at just one location. Many cardinals are attracted to this single location, and numerous interactions occur. However, even at feeders, cardinals engage in fewer encounters than might be expected, and the encounters that do occur are usually limited to a quick display. Only infrequently do cardinals actually fight. This is because cardinals usually recognize their status or rank relative to others, and to avoid wasting energy and possible injury, lower-ranked individuals defer to higher-ranked individuals. When fights occur, it is often because two individuals have similar status and it is not clear which, if either, should defer to the other. Such fights are normally brief, with the individuals involved quickly determining their status relative to each other.

About 60 percent of adult cardinals survive from one year to the next—in other words, about 40 percent of adult cardinals die each year. As noted in the last chapter, mortality rates for younger cardinals are even higher. Some of this mortality occurs during the breeding season, but it is likely that most deaths occur during the nonbreeding period.

Death can result from a variety of diseases and parasites. For example, feather parasites may reduce the insulating capacity of plumage, and the resulting loss of body heat may increase mortality during cold weather. Available evidence indicates that winter food supplies also affect survival rates in some areas. A study in North Carolina revealed that most of the seeds eaten by Northern Cardinals during the winter became scarce by mid-March. In addition, a correlation was found between cardinal numbers and food abundance. This suggests

that cardinals are limited by their winter food supply. If supplies run low, some cardinals must either disperse or die. Death may not result directly from starvation, but cardinals in poor condition are more likely to die in other ways. Weakened cardinals may spend more time in open areas looking for food, making them more likely to be spotted by predators. Also, a weakened cardinal is less able to elude a pursuing predator. High on the list of predators that prey on cardinals during the nonbreeding period are the accipiters or bird-eating hawks. Both Cooper's Hawks and Sharp-shinned Hawks prey primarily on songbirds, including cardinals. During the winter, many of these hawks move south from their breeding grounds and prey on numerous cardinals and other songbirds. Another predator that occasionally preys on cardinals is the Eastern Screech–Owl. Screech–Owls are nocturnal and sometimes take cardinals from their nighttime roosts. These owls sometimes become active before sunset and probably observe birds as they go to their nightly roosts.

Other predators that occasionally prey on cardinals include other hawks and some predatory mammals, such as minks, weasels, and foxes. In urban and suburban areas, domestic cats may be the primary predators of songbirds, including cardinals. One investigator estimated that domestic cats in North America kill over one billion birds every year.

11

Relations with Humans

Northern Cardinals, like all species of birds, can be negatively affected by humans. For example, our destruction of forests in the eastern half of the United States has created suitable habitat for Brown-headed Cowbirds, which parasitize cardinal nests. Some impacts are more direct. Cardinals and other birds are sometimes hit by vehicles. The exact numbers are unknown, but it has been estimated that at least fifty-seven million birds, including many cardinals, are killed by vehicles in the United States each year.

In addition, cardinals are sometimes injured or die when they fly into windows. No doubt some cardinals also die from accidental exposure to pesticides. Few people are aware of this mortality because scavengers such as cats, dogs, opossums, and raccoons quickly remove most bird carcasses.

Fortunately, not all human impacts have been negative. Cardinals, perhaps more than many species of birds, have benefited from some human activities. For example, before the arrival of Europeans in North America, the edge or shrub habitats preferred by cardinals were less common than they are today. There was, however, an abundance of mature forest. Cardinals inhabit the forest interior, but their numbers in such habitats are typically lower than in edge habitats. As a result, cardinals were probably found at relatively low densities throughout much of their range (which, back then, did not extend as far north as it does now).

Before European settlement, cardinals were probably found in greater numbers in habitats with more shrubs and denser ground-level vegetation than deep within mature forests. Such habitats probably included the areas along streams and rivers, along cliff edges and ridges, and in and near any natural openings in the forest. Also, cardinals probably used temporary forest edges created by fire or insect outbreaks. Cardinals may have also benefited from the activities of Native Americans, taking advantage of the edge habitats created from abandoned cornfields, abandoned village sites, or fires used to clear areas of forest. With the arrival of Europeans, the clearing of eastern deciduous forests and the creation of edge habitats greatly accelerated. Today, much of eastern North America is dominated by edge habitats, with a patchwork of wooded areas interspersed with shrubs, pastures, urban and suburban areas, and agricultural fields. Because much of this area is good habitat for cardinals, it is likely that cardinals are more abundant now than during presettlement times.

In addition to massive habitat alteration, many people in eastern North American have, more recently, assisted cardinals and other birds by providing substantial amounts of food at feeding stations. Although there have been no studies of cardinals, studies of other resident species

revealed that supplemental feeding can improve a bird's condition and result in increased survivorship. Thus, cardinals with access to a feeding station may be in better condition and more likely to survive the winter than cardinals without such access. Cardinal populations may, therefore, be higher in areas where feeders are present than in areas where they are not. Feeding has a substantial impact on cardinal populations in many areas of North America, because increasing numbers of people are participating in this activity. A survey published in 1988 indicated that over eighty-two million people in the United States feed birds, and that number has almost certainly increased—perhaps substantially—since then.

Although it seems reasonable to conclude that habitat alterations over the last 200 years have caused cardinal populations to increase in the eastern United States, there are no supporting data. Until relatively recently, few people were interested in monitoring bird populations, and as a result, there is no way of knowing whether cardinal populations have increased, decreased, or remained stable since the arrival of Europeans. Only since 1966, with the beginning of the Breeding Bird Survey (BBS), has there been a systematic means of monitoring bird populations in North America. Analysis of data gathered from 1966 through 1993 indicates that cardinal populations in the United States and Canada have remained stable. In contrast, the populations of many other species, particularly some grassland species and a variety of Neotropical migrants, have declined. Cardinals have at least two advantages over many other songbirds. First, cardinals are not migratory and are not affected by such things as habitat destruction in Central or South America. Second, cardinals have rather broad habitat requirements and can do well in urban or suburban areas. Thus, cardinal populations may be less affected by urbanization or other habitat alteration than those of many other species of birds.

In part because cardinals can occupy such a diversity of habitats, attracting cardinals is a simple matter throughout much of their range. A feeder regularly filled with sunflower seeds should bring in any nearby cardinals, after allowing several days for the birds to find it. Just about any type of feeder will attract cardinals, including ground feeders, platform feeders, post feeders, and hanging feeders. Ground or platform feeders are probably preferred by cardinals, but the other types are used as well. Cardinals are most easily attracted to feeders, and attracted in greater numbers, during the winter, but they continue to visit feeders throughout the year. Once territories are established in the spring, however, it is likely that fewer cardinals will visit a feeder, because the feeder will become part of one pair's territory, and that pair will do its best to keep other cardinals away. Occasionally, neighboring or nonbreeding individuals may elude the territorial pair and make their way to the feeder.

At feeding stations, cardinals prefer oil-type sunflower seeds but are also fond of black-striped and gray-striped sunflower seeds. Although sunflower seeds are always preferred, cardinals occasionally eat other seeds. In one study, several types of seeds were simultaneously offered to cardinals at different feeders, and investigators compared the frequency of visits to the feeder with black-striped sunflower seeds to the frequency of visits to feeders with other types of seeds. Thus, a rating (or ratio) of 1 would indicate that a feeder stocked with a particular type of seed was visited as frequently as the feeder with black-striped sunflower seeds, and a rating of 0.5 would indicate half as many visits. Using this system, oil-type sunflower seeds earned a rating of 1.14, gray-striped sunflower seeds 0.67, and hulled sunflower seeds 0.37. Other types of seeds had much lower ratings, indicating that cardinals ate them much less frequently. They included white proso millet, 0.20; red proso millet, 0.14; milo, 0.12; new wheat, 0.11; peanut kernels, 0.07; old wheat, 0.07; fine cracked corn, 0.06; german millet, 0.06; peanut hearts, 0.04; and niger, 0.02.

A well-stocked feeding station will attract cardinals and provide brief glimpses of some of the behaviors described in preceding chapters. Providing cardinals with other important requirements, such as protective cover, nest sites, natural foods, and a source of water, will permit more prolonged, and varied, observations.

Water can be just as attractive to cardinals and other birds as food. In the drier areas of North America, during prolonged dry spells just about anywhere, and during extended periods of subfreezing temperatures in winter, water is a scarce resource. Cardinals get some water from their food, particularly during the warmer months, when insects are an important part of their diet, but cardinals always require access to water for drinking and bathing. Water can be provided in a number of ways, from an upside-down garbage can lid to an in-ground pool or pond. Of course, a wide variety of birdbaths are also available for purchase. Most important is to make sure that the water container—whether it is a lid, a birdbath, a pool, or something else—provides a gradual incline into the water and that it is always (or almost always) filled with water. During northern winters, water can be kept ice free by using water heaters, which are available commercially.

Planting trees, shrubs, and vines that provide food, shelter, and nest sites can also attract cardinals. Appropriate species vary with geographical location, but at any location, cardinals prefer dense shrubs and vines for roosting and nesting. In many areas, eastern red cedars provide roosting and nesting sites, especially early in the breeding season, when deciduous vegetation has not yet developed leaves. Other plants that can provide good cover include junipers, American holly, and hawthorns. Grapevines also provide good cover, and female cardinals like to use grape bark when constructing nests. Cardinals also eat grape seeds. Other plants that provide food for cardinals include dogwoods, blackberries, and hackberries. A variety of so-called weeds can also be important sources of food for cardinals. These include doveweeds, knotweeds, ragweeds, foxtail, lamb's-quarters, crabgrass, and sedges. Although not appreciated by most people, these and other weeds produce large numbers of seeds and are valuable to cardinals and other seed-eating birds.

References

Andersen, M. E., and R. N. Conner. 1985. Northern Cardinal song in three forest habitats in eastern Texas.*Wilson Bull.* 97:436–49.

Beissinger, S. R., and D. R. Osborne. 1982. Effects of urbanization on avian community structure. *Condor* 84:75–83.

Bent, A. C. 1968. *Life histories of North American cardinals, grosbeaks, buntings, towhees, finches, sparrows and allies.* Part 1. New York: Dover Publications.

Best, L. B., and J. P. Gionfriddo. 1991. Characterization of grit use by cornfield birds. *Wilson Bull.* 103:68–82.

Bock, W. J. 1966. An approach to the functional analysis of bill shape. *Auk* 83:10–51.

Booth, L. M. 1980. Reproductive success of the cardinal in relation to territory size and arthropod availability in three eastern Texas forests. Master's thesis, Stephen F. Austin State University, Nacogdoches, TX.

Burns, R. D. 1963. Michigan cooperative cardinal study: nest data. *Jack-Pine Warbler* 41:56–61.

Choudhury, S. 1995. Divorce in birds: a review of the hypotheses. *Anim. Behav.* 50:413–29.

Conner, R. N., M. E. Anderson, and J. G. Dickson. 1986. Relationships among territory size, habitat, song, and nesting success of Northern Cardinals. *Auk* 103:23–31.

Dawson, W. R. 1958. Relation of oxygen consumption and evaporative water loss to temperature in the cardinal. *Physiol. Zool.* 31:37–48.

Dittus, W. P. J., and R. E. Lemon. 1969. Effects of song tutoring and acoustic isolation on the song repertoires of cardinals. *Anim. Behav.* 17:523–33.

Dow, D. D. 1969a. Habitat utilization by cardinals in central and peripheral breeding populations. *Can. J. Zool.* 47:409–17.

Dow, D. D. 1969b. Home range and habitat of the cardinal in peripheral and central populations. *Can. J. Zool.* 47:103–14.

Dow, D. D. 1970. Distribution and dispersal of the cardinal in relation to vegetational cover and river systems. *Amer. Midl. Nat.* 84:198–207.

Dow, D. D., and D. M. Scott. 1971. Dispersal and range expansion by the cardinal: an analysis of banding records. *Can. J. Zool.* 49:185–98.

Dunn, E. H. 1993. Bird mortality from striking residential windows in winter. *J. Field Ornithol.* 64:302–9.

Eckerle, K. P., and R. Breitwisch. 1997. Reproductive success of the Northern Cardinal, a large host of Brown-headed Cowbirds. *Condor* 99:169–178.

Ehrhart, R. L., and R. N. Conner. 1986. Habitat selection by the Northern Cardinal in three eastern Texas forest stands. *Southwest. Natur.* 31:191–99.

Ehrlich, P. R., D. S. Dobkin, and D. Wheye. 1986. The adaptive significance of anting. *Auk* 103:835.

Filliater, T. S., and R. Breitwisch. 1997. Nestling provisioning by the extremely dichromatic Northern Cardinal (*Cardinalis cardinalis*). *Wilson Bull.* 109:145–153.

Filliater, T. S., R. Breitwisch, and P. M. Nealen. 1994. Predation on Northern Cardinal nests: does choice of nest site matter? *Condor* 96:761–68.

Filliater-Lee, T. S. 1992. Parental roles in feeding nestlings, and nest sites and nest success in Northern Cardinals. Master's thesis, University of Dayton, Dayton, OH.

Fitch, H. S. 1958. Home ranges, territories, and seasonal movements of vertebrates of the Natural History Reservation. *Univ. Kansas Publ. Mus. Nat. Hist.* 11:63–326.

Friedmann, H. 1971. Further information on the host relations of the parasitic cowbirds. *Auk* 88:239–55.

Geis, A. D. 1980. *Relative attractiveness of different foods at wild bird feeders.* Special Science Report–Wildlife no. 233. Washington, DC: U.S. Department of the Interior.

Gould, P. J. 1961. Territorial relationships between cardinals and Pyrrhuloxias. *Condor* 63:246–56.

Grubb, T. C., Jr., T. A. Waite, and A. J. Wiseman. 1991. Ptilochronology: induced feather growth in Northern Cardinals varies with age, sex, ambient temperature, and day length. *Wilson Bull.* 103:435–45.

Halkin, S. L. 1990. Singing from the nest: intrapair communication in cardinals. Ph.D. diss., University of Wisconsin, Madison.

Hill, G. E. 1992. Proximate basis of variation in carotenoid pigmentation in male House Finches. *Auk* 109:1–12.

Hill, G. E. 1994. Trait elaboration via adaptive mate choice: sexual conflict in the evolution of signals of male quality. *Ethol. Ecol. Evol.* 6:351–70.

Hodges, J. 1949. A study of the cardinal in Iowa. *Proc. Iowa Acad. Sci.* 56:347–61.

Hodson, N. L., and D. W. Snow. 1965. The road deaths enquiry, 1960–1961. *Bird Study* 12:90–99.

Hogstedt, G. 1983. Adaptation unto death: function of fear screams. *Am. Nat.* 121:562–70.

Holcomb, L. C. 1966. The development of grasping and balancing coordination in nestlings of seven species of altricial birds. *Wilson Bull.* 78:57–63.

Kinser, G. W. 1973. Ecology and behavior of the cardinal in southern Indiana. Ph.D. diss., Indiana University, Bloomington.

Klem, D., Jr. 1989. Bird-window collisions. *Wilson Bull.* 101:606–20.

Klem, D., Jr. 1990. Collisions between birds and windows: mortality and prevention. *J. Field Ornithol.* 61:120–28.

Kroodsma, R. L. 1984. Effect of edge on breeding forest bird species. *Wilson Bull.* 96:426–36.

Laskey, A. R. 1944. A study of the cardinal in Tennessee. *Wilson Bull.* 56:27–44.

Lemon, R. E. 1966. Geographic variation in the song of cardinals. *Can. J. Zool.* 44:413–28.

Lemon, R. E. 1967. The response of cardinals to songs of different dialects. *Anim. Behav.* 15:538–45.

Lemon, R. E. 1968a. The displays and call notes of cardinals. *Can. J. Zool.* 46:141–51.

Lemon, R. E. 1968b. The relation between organization and function of song in cardinals. *Behaviour* 32:158–78.

Lemon, R. E. 1975. How birds develop song dialects. *Condor* 77:385–406.

Lemon, R. E., and A. Herzog. 1969. The vocal behavior of cardinals and Pyrrhuloxias in Texas. *Condor* 71:1–15.

Lemon, R. E., and D. M. Scott. 1966. On the development of song in young cardinals. *Can. J. Zool.* 44:191–97.

Lever, C. 1987. *Naturalized birds of the world.* New York: Wiley and Sons.

Martin, T. E., and P. Li. 1992. Life history traits of open- vs. cavity-nesting birds. *Ecology* 73:579–92.

McAtee, W. L. 1908. *Food habits of the grosbeaks.* U.S. Department of Agriculture Bull. no. 32. Washington, DC: Government Printing Office.

McElroy, D. B., and G. Ritchison. 1996. Effect of mate removal on singing behavior and movement patterns of female Northern Cardinals. *Wilson Bull.* 108:550–55

Mobley, J. E., Jr. 1994. A general model for iteroparity: development of the model and investigation of phylogenetic patterns with specific reference to the Northern Cardinal. Ph.D. diss., University of Arkansas, Fayetteville.

Nolan, V., Jr. 1963. Reproductive success of birds in a deciduous scrub habitat. *Ecology* 44:305–14.

Parrish, J. W., J. A. Ptacek, and K. L. Will. 1984. The detection of near-ultraviolet light by nonmigratory and migratory birds. *Auk* 101:53–58.

Petit, D. R., and L. J. Petit. 1987. Fecal sac dispersal by Prothonotary Warblers: Weatherhead's hypothesis re-evaluated. *Condor* 89:610–13.

Potter, E. F. 1970. Anting in wild birds, its frequency and probable purpose. *Auk* 87:692–713.

Pressman, D. S. 1987. The songs of female Northern Cardinals: development, description, and influence of exposure to a singing male. Master's thesis, Eastern Kentucky University, Richmond.

Price, J., S. Droege, and A. Price. 1995. *The summer atlas of North American birds.* New York: Academic Press.

Pulliam, H. R., and F. Enders. 1971. The feeding ecology of five sympatric finch species. *Ecology* 52:557–66.

Reese, J. G. 1975. Fall remex and rectrix molt in the cardinal. *Bird-Banding* 46:305–10.

Richmond, A. 1978. An experimental study of advantages of monogamy in the cardinal. Ph.D. diss., Indiana University, Bloomington.

Ritchison, G. 1986. The singing behavior of female Northern Cardinals. *Condor* 88:156–59.

Ritchison, G. 1988. Song repertoires and the singing behavior of male Northern Cardinals. *Wilson Bull.* 100:583–603.

Ritchison, G., P. H. Klatt, and D. F. Westneat. 1994. Mate guarding and extra-pair paternity in Northern Cardinals. *Condor* 96:1055–63.

Ritchison, G., and M. K. Omer. 1990. Winter behavior of Northern Cardinals. *Trans. Ky. Acad. Sci.* 51:145–53.

Root, T. L. 1988. Atlas of wintering North American birds: an analysis of Christmas bird count data. Chicago: University Chicago Press.

Scott, D. M., and R. E. Lemon. 1996. Differential reproductive success of Brown-headed Cowbirds with Northern Cardinals and three other hosts. *Condor* 98:259–71.

Scott, D.M., R. E. Lemon, and J. A. Darley. 1987. Relaying interval after nest failure in Gray Catbirds and Northern Cardinals. *Wilson Bull.* 99:708–12.

Shaver, J. M., and M. B. Roberts. 1930. Some nesting habits of the cardinal. *J. Tenn. Acad. Sci.* 5:157–70.

Shaver, J. M., and M. B. Roberts. 1933. A brief study of the courtship of the eastern cardinal. J. *Tenn. Acad. Sci.* 8:116–23.

Sheppard, D. H., P. H. Klopfer, and H. Oelke. 1968. Habitat selection: differences in stereotype between insular and continental birds. *Wilson Bull.* 80:452–57.

Shuman, T. W., R. J. Robel, J. L. Zimmerman, and K. E. Kemp. 1989. Variance in digestive efficiencies of four sympatric avian granivores. *Auk* 106:324–26.

Stone, W. B., S. R. Overmann, and J. C. Okoniewski. 1984. Intentional poisoning of birds with parathion. *Condor* 86:333–36.

Thompson, C. W., and M. Leu. 1994. Determining homology of molts and plumages to address evolutionary questions: a rejoinder regarding emberizid finches. *Condor* 96:769–82.

Williams, M. K. 1986. Winter behavior of the Northern Cardinal. Master's thesis, Eastern Kentucky University, Richmond.

Willson, M. F. 1972. Seed size preference in finches. *Wilson Bull.* 84:449–55.

Willson, M. F., and J. C. Harmeson. 1973. Seed preferences and digestive efficiency of cardinals and Song Sparrows. *Condor* 75:225–34.

Wilson, W. H., Jr. 1994. The distribution of wintering birds in central Maine: the interactive effects of landscape and bird feeders. *J. Field Ornithol.* 65:512–19.

Wiseman, A. J. 1977. Interrelation of variables in postjuvenal molt of cardinals. *Bird-Banding* 48:206–23.

Wolfenbarger, L. L. 1996. Fitness effects associated with red coloration of male Northern Cardinals. Ph.D. diss., Cornell University, Ithaca, NY.

Yen, C. W. 1989. A plumage study of the cardinal of western Pennsylvania. *Bull. Nat. Mus. Nat. Sci.* 1:11–21.

Photo Credits

Page 54
Steve Maslowski/
Maslowski Photo (top)
Dave Dvorak, Jr.
(bottom)

Page 55
Leonard Lee Rue III
(top)

Page 56
Steve Maslowski/
Maslowski Photo (top)
Gerard Lemmo
(bottom)

Page 57
Steve Maslowski/
Maslowski Photo (top)
Steve Maslowski/
Maslowski Photo
(bottom)

Page 58
Tom Ulrich (top)
Richard Day/Daybreak
Imagery (bottom)

Page 59
Bill Duyck

Page 60
Bill Duyck (top)
Steve Maslowski/
Maslowski Photo
(bottom)

Page 61
Rich Kirchner/The
Green Agency

Page 62
Bill Duyck (top)
Bill Duyck (bottom)

Page 63
Jim Roetzel

Page 64
Doug Locke

Page 66
Rich Kirchner/The
Green Agency (top)
Jim Roetzel (bottom)

Page 67
Gary W. Carter

Page 68
Bill Duyck

Page 69
Bill Duyck

Page 70
Richard Day/Daybreak
Imagery (top)
Bill Duyck (bottom)

Page 71
Richard Day/Daybreak
Imagery

Page 72
Richard Day/Daybreak
Imagery

Page 73
Gerard Lemmo

Page 74
Gary W. Carter (top)
Bill Duyck (bottom)

Page 75
Bill Duyck

Page 76
Bill Duyck (top)
Bill Duyck (bottom)

Page 77
Leonard Lee Rue III

Page 78
Gerard Lemmo

Page 79
Bill Duyck (top)
Richard Day/Daybreak
Imagery (bottom)

Page 80
Bill Duyck (top)
Steve Maslowski/
Maslowski Photo
(bottom)

Page 81
Leonard Lee Rue III

Page 82
Gregory Scott

Page 83
Richard Day/Daybreak
Imagery (top)
Richard Day/Daybreak
Imagery (bottom)

Page 84
Gregory Scott

Page 85
Richard Day/Daybreak
Imagery

Page 86
Richard Day/Daybreak
Imagery

Page 87
Steve Maslowski/
Maslowski Photo

Page 88
Steve Maslowski/
Maslowski Photo

Page 89
Steve Maslowski/
Maslowski Photo

Page 90
Steve Maslowski/
Maslowski Photo (top)
Jim Roetzel (bottom)

Page 91
Steve Maslowski/
Maslowski Photo

Page 92
Tom Vezo

Page 93
Steve Maslowski/
Maslowski Photo (top)
Steve Maslowski/
Maslowski Photo
(bottom)

Page 94
Russell Hansen

Page 95
Tom Vezo

Page 96
Steve Maslowski/
Maslowski Photo (top)
J.R. Woodward/VIREO

Page 97
C. Allan Morgan (top)
Steve Maslowski/
Maslowski Photo
(bottom)

Page 98
James H. Robinson

Page 99
Russell Hansen

Page 100
Steve Bentsen

Page 101
Steve Maslowski/
Maslowski Photo

Page 102
James H. Robinson

Page 103
Ron Morreim

Page 104
Steve Maslowski/
Maslowski Photo

Page 105
Steve Maslowski/
Maslowski Photo (top)
Steve Maslowski/
Maslowski Photo
(bottom)

Page 106
Ron Morreim

Page 107
Steve Maslowski/
Maslowski Photo (top)
Tom Vezo (bottom)

Page 108
Richard Day/Daybreak
Imagery

Page 109
Richard Day/Daybreak
Imagery

Page 110
Steve Maslowski/
Maslowski Photo (top)
Steve Maslowski/
Maslowski Photo
(bottom)

Page 111
Steve Maslowski/
Maslowski Photo

Page 112
Richard Day/Daybreak
Imagery

Page 113
Charles Melton

Page 114
Leonard Lee Rue III

Page 115
Steve Maslowski/
Maslowski Photo

About the Author

Gary Ritchison is a professor of Biological Sciences at Eastern Kentucky University. He has published in numerous ornithological journals and has presented papers to several academic societies on behavior and ecology of a variety of bird species, including Northern Cardinals. He lives in Richmond, Kentucky.